CKD STAGE 4 AND TYPE 2

DIABETES

COOKBOOK

Beginners Guide to Diabetic Renal Diet with Low Sodium, Low Potassium and Low Carb Recipes to Manage Kidney Disease and Blood Sugar Level

ANGELA R. STATEN

Copyright© 2024 by **Angela R. Staten**

All rights reserved. No part of this publication may be reproduced,

distributed, or transmitted in any form or by any means, including

photocopying, recording, or other electronic or mechanical methods,

without the prior written permission of the publisher, except in the case

of brief quotations embodied in critical reviews and certain other

noncommercial uses permitted by copyright la

TABLE OF CONTENTS

ABOUT THE AUTHOR

My name is Angela Rachel Staten, and I'm a medical professional and qualified nutritionist who is totally committed to using food as medicine.

Although it may sound generic, I have personally witnessed the profound impact that a healthy diet can have on people's lives.

I am a case study in action.

Whether you have kidney disease or are facing diabetes, my intention is not to give you a ton of confusing guidelines.

Rather, I wish to provide you with the means to effect long-term change.

One of the greatest methods to achieve this is by following a healthy diet, which focuses on eating tasty but simple foods that will fuel your body and provide you with the strongest defense against illness.

You will find in this book:

Clear explanations of the nutritional value of food and how it affects leading a healthy lifestyle.

scrumptious meals that genuinely inspire a desire for healthy eating.

Some pointers for incorporating this diet into your busy lifestyle.

Consider myself your companion in this. One delectable, nutritious meal at a time, I'm here to help you on your path to feeling better.

So unwind and let's get star

INTRODUCTION

Have you been told you have both CKD Stage 4 and Type 2 diabetes? Does the endless list of "don't eat this" and "limit that" make every meal feel like a minefield? Are you frustrated by cookbooks that focus on one condition but not the unique challenges of managing both?

If so, you're not alone. Navigating the world of kidney-friendly and diabetes-friendly eating is no easy feat.

It might feel like everything you used to enjoy is suddenly off-limits. And it's not just about the food – it's about your health, your quality of life, and the worry that hangs over every bite.

However, things don't have to be this way.

This cookbook is designed specifically for you. It's your guide to creating delicious, satisfying meals that nourish your body without sacrificing flavor or variety.

Inside, you'll find:

Clear explanations of how your diet impacts both CKD and diabetes, empowering you to make informed choices.

Practical tips for stocking your pantry and mastering the basics of a kidney- and diabetes-friendly kitchen.

Recipes that celebrate taste, not restrictions – from comforting breakfasts to vibrant salads and satisfying main courses.

Meal planning guidance to help you balance blood sugar levels and protect your kidneys.

This isn't about deprivation; it's about discovering new possibilities. Consider this your roadmap to a way of eating that supports your health and makes meals something to look forward to again.

Let's get cooking!

Understanding CKD and Diabetes

Imagine your kidneys as super filters, constantly cleaning your blood. In CKD, these filters become damaged over time, making it harder for them to remove waste products and excess fluids from your body.

At stage 4, your kidneys are working at only about 15-30% of their normal capacity. This can lead to a buildup of toxins in your blood, which can affect your bones, heart, and overall health.

Symptoms to watch out for:

- Feeling more tired than usual
- Difficulty sleeping
- Loss of appetite
- Puffiness around your eyes or ankles
- High blood pressure
- Changes in how often you urinate or the amount of urine

Type 2 Diabetes:

This is a condition where your body struggles to use insulin, a hormone that helps regulate blood sugar levels. When insulin isn't working properly, sugar builds up in your bloodstream instead of being used for energy.

How it affects your body:

Over time, high blood sugar can damage your nerves, blood vessels, and organs, leading to complications like heart disease, vision problems, and nerve pain.

Symptoms to be aware of:

- Frequent urination
- Increased thirst
- Feeling very hungry (even after eating)
- Unexplained weight loss
- Fatigue

- Blurred vision

The Link Between CKD and Diabetes

These conditions often go hand-in-hand. Having diabetes can increase your risk of developing CKD, and CKD can make it harder to control your blood sugar. It's like a double whammy for your kidneys.

Don't panic!

Early diagnosis and management are crucial, and this book is here to empower you on that journey. By understanding how these conditions work and making smart food choices, you can take control of your health and feel better.

The Importance of Diet:

Diet plays a pivotal role in managing both Chronic Kidney Disease (CKD) and type 2 diabetes, going far beyond simple blood sugar control.

When tailored carefully, the way you eat becomes a powerful tool to protect kidney function, maintain healthy blood sugar levels, and support overall well-being.

Let's break down the key areas where diet makes a difference:

Kidney Protection: In CKD Stage 4, focusing on specific nutrients lessens the workload on your kidneys. This includes:

Sodium (Salt): Excess sodium raises blood pressure, a major risk for further kidney damage. A low-sodium diet helps control blood pressure and reduces fluid buildup.

Potassium: With damaged kidneys, potassium can build up in the blood. Managing potassium sources is vital to prevent heart rhythm issues.

Phosphorus: High phosphorus strains the kidneys and compromises bone health.

Protein: Balancing protein intake is crucial. Too little risks malnutrition, while too much taxes the kidneys' waste-filtering abilities.

Blood Sugar Control: For those with type 2 diabetes:

Carbohydrates: The right types and amounts of carbs help stabilize blood sugar spikes. This means prioritizing whole grains, fruits, and vegetables while limiting sugary foods and refined starches.

Healthy Fats: These promote satiety and slow carbohydrate digestion, further aiding blood sugar control.

Meal Timing: Regular, balanced meals prevent large fluctuations in blood sugar throughout the day.

Diet does more than just manage only CKD and Diabetes it also help with the following

Inflammation: Certain foods increase inflammation, putting stress on the body. An anti-inflammatory way of eating fights this, protecting overall health.

Heart Health: Many kidney- and diabetes-friendly dietary recommendations overlap with those for a healthy heart, reducing cardiovascular risks.

Weight Management: Achieving a healthy weight lessens the burden on both your kidneys and your blood sugar regulation.

Quality of Life: Nourishing your body with delicious, satisfying foods makes this way of eating sustainable and enjoyable, crucial for long-term success.

Your Cookbook as a Guide:

This cookbook is more than recipes. It's your roadmap to creating a dietary pattern that empowers you to take charge of both your CKD and diabetes. You'll learn how to make mindful food choices, discover flavor without compromising your health, and achieve the confidence that comes with taking control.

CHAPTER 1

THE FOUNDATIONS OF YOUR KIDNEY- AND DIABETES-FRIENDLY KITCHEN

Key Nutrients to Focus On

Managing CKD stage 4 and type 2 diabetes requires careful attention to your diet. Here's a breakdown of key nutrients and why they matter:

Protein:Protein is necessary for the synthesis and maintenance of bodily tissue.

However, with CKD, the kidneys have reduced ability to filter waste products from protein breakdown. Generally speaking, moderate protein consumption is advised (for CKD stage 4).

General Daily Intake: 0.6 - 0.8 gram of protein per kilogram of body weight.

Consult your doctor for your specific needs.

Carbohydrates: Carbohydrates are your body's primary energy source.

Type 2 diabetes affects how your body processes carbohydrates, leading to fluctuating blood sugar levels. Prioritize complex carbohydrates like whole grains, fruits, and vegetables over simple sugars. Portion control is important for blood sugar management.

General Daily Intake: Recommendations vary. Discuss with your dietitian to create a personalized carbohydrate goal.

Sodium: Sodium helps regulate fluid balance. However, excess sodium strains damage the kidneys and worsens blood pressure. Focus on fresh, unprocessed foods, and limit the use of table salt.

General Daily Intake: Aim for less than 2,300 mg of sodium per day. Individual needs may be lower.

Potassium: The heart and muscles depend on potassium for proper operation.

CKD can disrupt potassium balance. Your doctor may recommend limiting high-potassium foods like bananas, potatoes, and tomatoes.

General Daily Intake: Recommendations vary. Your doctor or dietitian will provide a specific target.

Phosphorus: Phosphorus helps build healthy bones. Damaged kidneys have difficulty filtering excess phosphorus. Limit processed foods, certain dairy products, and some protein sources high in phosphorus.

General Daily Intake: Aim for 800-1000 mg of phosphorus per day, or lower depending on your doctor's guidance.

Fluids: Fluids are essential, but intake may need to be restricted in advanced CKD. Your doctor will recommend the right fluid balance for you.

Food to manage both condition

Category	Low-Potassium Options	High-Fiber Options (Moderation)
Vegetables	Cauliflower, broccoli, cabbage, carrots, green beans, cucumbers,	Brussels sprouts, asparagus, green peas
	peppers, onions, garlic, eggplant, lettuce, arugula, zucchini	
Fruits	Berries, apples, pears, grapes (in moderation)	
Lean Meats	Chicken, turkey (without skin), lean cuts of beef or pork	
Fish	Salmon, tuna, cod, tilapia	
Eggs	Egg whites (preferred), whole eggs (in moderation)	
Plant-Based	Tofu, tempeh, edamame, lentils (in moderation)	
Grains	Brown rice, quinoa, oats, whole wheat bread (in moderation)	
Dairy	Unsweetened almond milk, rice milk, or soy milk	Greek yogurt
Healthy Fats	Olive oil, avocado oil, avocados, nuts, seeds (in moderation)	
Herbs	Basil, bay leaves, cilantro, chives	
Spices	Allspice, black pepper, cardamom, chili powder, cinnamon	
Other	Water (6-8 glasses per day)	

Foods to Limit or Avoid

Category	High Potassium	High Sugar/Carbohydrates	High Sodium	High Phosphorus
Fruits	Bananas, oranges, cantaloupe, honeydew, dried fruits,	Canned fruit in syrup, fruit juices, fruit punch		
	avocados, pomegranate, coconut, mangoes, nectarines			
Vegetables	Potatoes, sweet potatoes, tomatoes, winter squash,		Canned vegetables, pickled vegetables, sauerkraut	
	beets, pumpkin, Swiss chard, artichokes			
Protein Sources			Cured meats, deli meats, fast food, frozen breaded items	Processed meats, organ meats, canned fish
				dairy products

Grains		White bread, white rice, refined pasta,		
		sugary cereals, pastries, cakes, cookies, crackers		
Dairy				Milk, cheese, yogurt
Other		Candy, sugary drinks, desserts, sweetened yogurt	Table salt, soy sauce, processed foods, fast food	Chocolate, colas

Ckd stage 4 and type 2 diabetes food list

Category	Recommended Foods	Foods to Limit or Avoid (Moderation or with Caution)	Foods to Avoid
Fruits	Apples, berries, grapes (moderation), pears	Bananas, oranges, cantaloupe, honeydew melon, dried fruits, avocados	Canned fruits in syrup, fruit juices, fruit punch
Vegetables	Asparagus, broccoli, Brussels sprouts, cabbage, carrots,	Potatoes, sweet potatoes, tomatoes, winter squash, beets, pumpkin	Canned/pickled vegetables, sauerkraut
	cauliflower, celery, cucumbers, eggplant, green beans, garlic,		
	lettuce, onions, peppers, summer squash, zucchini		
Protein	Chicken (skinless), fish (salmon, tuna in water, cod, tilapia),	Processed meats (bacon, sausage, hot dogs), organ meats, canned fish	
	lean beef/pork, egg whites (whole eggs in moderation), tofu,	with bones,	
	tempeh, edamame		

Grains	Brown rice, quinoa, oats, whole wheat bread (limit portion sizes)	White rice, refined pasta, white bread, sugary cereals, pastries, cookies	
Dairy	Unsweetened almond milk, rice milk, soy milk	Milk, cheese, yogurt (except small amounts of plain, non-fat Greek yogurt)	
Fats	Olive oil, avocado oil, avocados		
Herbs & Spices	Basil, bay leaves, cilantro, chives, dill, mint, oregano,		
	parsley, rosemary, sage, tarragon, thyme		
	Allspice, black pepper, cardamom, chili powder, cinnamon,		
	cloves, cumin, curry powder, garlic powder, ginger, nutmeg,		
	onion powder, paprika, turmeric		

Essential Kitchen Tools

Must-Have Tools:

Measuring Tools: Precise measuring is crucial for portion control and managing nutrient intake. Invest in a good set of measuring cups and spoons, as well as a kitchen scale for weighing ingredients.

Sharp Knives: A chef's knife, paring knife, and serrated knife make chopping, slicing, and dicing easier and safer. This helps with meal preparation efficiency and reduces the risk of accidents.

Cutting Boards: Have separate cutting boards for meat and produce to prevent cross-contamination. Choose non-porous materials for easy cleaning.

Pots and Pans: A variety of sizes will be useful for different recipes. Non-stick options make cooking and cleaning easier.

Baking Sheet: Ideal for roasting vegetables, baking fish or chicken, and even making low-sugar desserts.

Mixing Bowls: A set of mixing bowls in various sizes allows for easy preparation of salads, marinades, and sauces.

Colander: Essential for draining pasta, rinsing vegetables, and washing fruits.

Vegetable Peeler: Helps remove the skin from fruits and vegetables, which can be helpful for reducing potassium intake.

Steamer Basket: Steaming is a healthy cooking method that preserves nutrients and flavor.

Blender or Food Processor: These appliances can help you make smoothies, soups, sauces, and purees.

Storage Containers: Glass or BPA-free plastic containers are ideal for storing leftovers and prepped ingredients.

CHAPTER 2

MEAL PLANNING MADE EASY

Balancing Blood Sugar

Maintaining stable blood sugar levels is crucial for individuals managing both CKD stage 4 and type 2 diabetes. Here's a medically-informed approach to structuring meals for optimal glycemic control:

Meal Composition:

Carbohydrate Distribution: Instead of consuming large amounts of carbohydrates at once, distribute them evenly throughout the day. Aim for 3-4 small meals and 1-2 snacks, spacing them out every 2-3 hours. This lessens the likelihood of blood sugar surges and crashes.

Focus on Complex Carbohydrates: Prioritize complex carbohydrates like whole grains, legumes, and non-starchy vegetables. These provide sustained energy and are digested slower than simple sugars, resulting in more stable blood glucose levels.

Protein Inclusion: Incorporate lean protein sources like chicken, fish, tofu, or eggs in every meal and snack. Protein slows down digestion and helps stabilize blood sugar levels.

Healthy Fats: Include healthy fats like olive oil, avocados, and nuts in moderation.

These fats can help improve insulin sensitivity and slow down the absorption of carbohydrates.

Fiber Intake: High-fiber foods like fruits, vegetables, and whole grains are essential. Fiber slows down digestion, promoting better blood sugar control. However, be mindful of the potassium content in some high-fiber foods if you have CKD.

Practical Tips:

Monitor Blood Glucose: Regularly check your blood sugar levels before and after meals to identify patterns and make adjustments as needed.

Mindful Eating: Pay attention to hunger and fullness cues. Avoid skipping meals or overeating.

Hydration: Drink plenty of water throughout the day. High blood sugar levels might result from dehydration.

Regular Exercise: Engaging in regular physical activity helps improve insulin sensitivity and lower blood sugar levels.

Limit Processed Foods: These foods are often high in added sugar, unhealthy fats, and sodium, which can negatively impact blood sugar control and kidney function.

Consult Your Doctor: Work with your healthcare provider to develop an individualized meal plan that takes into account your specific needs and health conditions.

Kidney-Protective Portions

Optimal nutrition plays a crucial role in managing chronic kidney disease (CKD) and preventing further decline in kidney function. Maintaining appropriate portion sizes and protein intake are essential components of a kidney-protective diet.

Protein Intake:

Individuals with CKD stage 4 often require a moderate protein restriction to reduce the workload on the kidneys. The recommended daily protein intake varies depending on individual factors such as age, weight, and residual kidney function. Generally, 0.8 grams of protein per kilogram of body weight is recommended for CKD stage 4 patients not on dialysis. However, consulting a registered dietitian is crucial to determine the precise protein needs for each individual.

Practical Tips for Managing Protein Intake:

Choose Lean Protein Sources: Opt for lean cuts of meat (e.g., skinless poultry, fish, lean beef), egg whites, and plant-based protein sources like tofu and legumes.

Limit High-Phosphorus Protein Sources: Restrict intake of red meat, organ meats, dairy products, and nuts due to their high phosphorus content, which can burden the kidneys.

Distribute Protein Intake Throughout the Day: Instead of consuming a large portion of protein in one meal, spread it out over three meals to optimize protein utilization and minimize stress on the kidneys.

Meal Sizes:

Along with managing protein intake, controlling portion sizes is vital for maintaining a healthy weight and blood sugar levels, especially for individuals with type 2 diabetes. It is recommended to aim for smaller, more frequent meals rather than large, heavy meals. This helps prevent blood sugar spikes and aids in better digestion.

Practical Tips for Managing Meal Sizes:

Use Smaller Plates and Bowls: This can help create the illusion of a fuller plate and prevent overeating.

Fill Half Your Plate with Vegetables: Non-starchy vegetables are low in calories, high in fiber, and rich in nutrients, making them an ideal choice for CKD patients.

Practice Mindful Eating: Pay attention to hunger and fullness cues. Eat slowly and savor each bite to prevent overconsumption.

Pre-Portion Snacks: Prepare snacks in advance to avoid mindless eating and ensure appropriate portion sizes.

Tips for Dining Out

Dining out with CKD stage 4 and type 2 diabetes can be enjoyable and stress-free with a little preparation and know-how. Here are some practical tips to help you make smart choices in restaurants:

Before You Go:

Research the Restaurant: Look up the menu online or call ahead to inquire about kidney-friendly options. Many restaurants are happy to accommodate dietary needs.

Plan Your Meal: Choose a few dishes that align with your dietary restrictions. This will help you avoid impulse decisions when you arrive.

Ask About Preparation Methods: Inquire about how dishes are prepared. Request grilled, baked, or steamed options over fried or breaded ones.

Check for Hidden Ingredients: Some sauces, dressings, and marinades can be high in sodium, potassium, or phosphorus. Ask for these on the side or request modifications if possible.

At the Restaurant:

Communicate Your Needs: Don't be afraid to inform your server about your dietary restrictions. They can often offer suggestions or make modifications to menu items.

Control Portions: Restaurant portions are often larger than recommended serving sizes. Ask for a half-portion or split a dish with a friend.

Skip the Salt Shaker: Avoid adding extra salt to your food. To improve flavor, use herbs and spices instead.

Choose Wisely at the Buffet: If it's a buffet, fill your plate with vegetables, lean protein, and fruit. Avoid processed foods, fried dishes, and sugary desserts.

Modify Your Order: Don't hesitate to ask for substitutions or modifications to make a dish more kidney-friendly. For example, request vegetables instead of fries or ask for dressing on the side.

Watch Your Drinks: Limit sugary beverages and alcohol, as they can raise blood sugar levels. Opt for water, unsweetened tea, or sparkling water instead.

Don't Be Afraid to Ask Questions: If you're unsure about an ingredient or preparation method, ask your server for clarification.

Measurement guide

Common Measurement Abbreviations:

Abbreviation	Description
Tsp	teaspoon
Tbsp.	tablespoon
fl oz	fluid ounce
C	Cup
Pt	Pint
Qt	Quart
gal	gallon
Oz	ounce
Lb	pound
G	gram
kg	kilogram
ml	milliliter
L	liter

Key Conversions

Measurement Type	Conversion	Approximate Conversion
Volume	1 tbsp = 3 tsp	
	1 fl oz = 2 tbsp	
	1 c = 8 fl oz = 16 tbsp	
	1 pt = 2 c	
	1 qt = 2 pt = 4 c	
	4 qt = 8 pt = 16 c = 1 gal	
Weight	1 oz = 28.35 g	
	1 lb = 16 oz = 453.59 g	
	1 kg = 1000 g = 2.2 lbs	
US to Metric	1 c = 236.59 ml	240 ml
	1 tsp = 4.93 ml	5 ml
	1 tbsp = 14.79 ml	15 ml

Practical Examples for CKD and Diabetes

Protein:

If your recommended protein intake is 60 grams per day, and you're having 3 meals, aim for about 20 grams of protein per meal.

A 3-ounce serving of cooked chicken breast contains roughly 26 grams of protein.

A ½ cup serving of cooked lentils contains about 9 grams of protein.

Carbohydrates:

If you're aiming for 30 grams of carbohydrates per meal, a ½ cup serving of cooked brown rice contains about 22 grams of carbohydrates.

A small apple contains about 19 grams of carbohydrates.

Potassium:

A medium banana contains about 422 mg of potassium. If your daily limit is 2,000 mg, you'll need to be mindful of other high-potassium foods in your diet.

Tips:

Use a Kitchen Scale: For the most accurate measurements, especially for protein and carbohydrates, use a kitchen scale.

CHAPTER 3

Breakfast recipes

BERRY CHIA SEED PUDDING WITH RICE MILK

Yields: 1 serving | **Prep Time**: 5 minutes | **Refrigeration Time**: 4 hours minimum

INGREDIENTS

- ½ cup frozen or fresh mixed berries (strawberries, blueberries, raspberries)
- ¼ cup chia seeds
- 1 cup unsweetened rice milk
- ½ teaspoon vanilla extract
- Spices: pinch of cinnamon (optional)

INSTRUCTIONS

1. In a jar or container, combine berries, chia seeds, rice milk, and vanilla extract.
2. Stir well to combine.
3. Refrigerate for at least 4 hours, or overnight, until thickened.
4. Stir before serving. Add more rice milk if needed to achieve desired consistency.

TIPS

- Use unsweetened rice milk to minimize carb intake.

- This recipe is naturally low in potassium, phosphorus, and sodium.

- If using frozen berries, ensure they are not packed in syrup, which could add unnecessary sugar.

- Chia seeds are a good source of fiber, which can help regulate blood sugar levels.

NUTRITIONAL FACTS

Calories: ~150 kcal

Protein: ~5g

Carbohydrates: ~15g

Fiber: ~10g

Potassium: ~100mg

Phosphorus: ~50mg

Sodium: ~10mg

BAKED APPLE WITH CINNAMON AND NUTMEG

Yields: 1 serving | **Prep Time**: 5 minutes | **Cooking Time:** 30-40 minutes

INGREDIENTS

- 1 medium apple (Granny Smith or Honeycrisp)
- ½ teaspoon ground cinnamon
- ¼ teaspoon ground nutmeg

INSTRUCTIONS

1. Preheat the oven to 350°F (175°C).
2. Core the apple, leaving the bottom intact to form a small cup.
3. In a small bowl, combine cinnamon and nutmeg.
4. Sprinkle the spice mixture inside the hollowed-out apple.
5. Place the apple in a baking dish and add a small amount of water to the bottom of the dish.
6. Bake for 30-40 minutes, or until tender.
7. Let cool slightly before serving.

TIPS

- Choose a low-potassium apple variety like Granny Smith or Honeycrisp.

- Cinnamon and nutmeg are naturally low in potassium, phosphorus, and sodium.

- Baking the apple helps to soften the fiber and make it easier to digest.

NUTRITIONAL FACTS

Calories: ~100 kcal

Protein: ~0.5g

Carbohydrates: ~25g

Fiber: ~4g

Potassium: ~195 mg

Phosphorus: ~11mg

Sodium: ~2mg

SCRAMBLED EGG WHITES WITH SPINACH AND HERBS

Yields: 1 serving | **Prep Time:** 5 minutes | **Cooking Time:** 5-7 minutes

INGREDIENTS

- 2 large egg whites(yolk separated)
- 1 cup fresh spinach, chopped
- 1 teaspoon olive oil
- Herbs: 1 tablespoon chopped fresh herbs (parsley, chives, basil)
- Spices: Pinch of black pepper

INSTRUCTIONS

1. In a nonstick pan set over a medium-high temperature, warm the olive oil.
2. Add chopped spinach and cook until wilted.
3. In a bowl, whisk egg whites and black pepper.
4. Pour egg whites into the pan with spinach.
5. Stir gently as the eggs cook, until softly scrambled.
6. Take off the heat and add the fresh herbs.

TIPS

- Use only egg whites to lower cholesterol and phosphorus content.

- Iron and vitamin K are both abundant in spinach.

- Fresh herbs add flavor without adding sodium.

NUTRITIONAL FACTS

Calories: ~80 kcal

Protein: ~10g

Carbohydrates: ~3g

Fiber: ~2g

Potassium: ~100mg

Phosphorus: ~50mg

Sodium: ~5mg

RASPBERRY AND RICE MILK SMOOTHIE

Yields: one serving | **Prep Time:** five minutes

INGREDIENTS

- 1 cup unsweetened frozen raspberries
- ½ cup unsweetened rice milk
- ¼ cup water
- ½ teaspoon vanilla extract
- Spices: pinch of ground cinnamon or ginger (optional)

INSTRUCTIONS

1. Combine all ingredients in a blender.
2. Blend until smooth and creamy.
3. Adjust consistency with additional water or rice milk, if desired.

TIPS

- This smoothie is a good source of antioxidants and vitamin C.
- If you prefer a sweeter taste, add a few drops of liquid stevia.
- You can adjust the amount of rice milk to achieve your desired consistency.

NUTRITIONAL FACTS

Calories: approximately 100

Protein: one gram

Carbohydrates: 20 grams

Fiber: four grams

Potassium: 150 milligrams

Phosphorus: 30 milligrams

Sodium: 10 milligrams

TOFU SCRAMBLE WITH TURMERIC AND VEGETABLES

Yields: two servings | **Prep Time:** 10 minutes | **Cooking Time:** 15 minutes

INGREDIENTS

- ½ block firm tofu, drained and crumbled
- 1 tablespoon olive oil
- ½ cup chopped onion
- ½ cup chopped green pepper
- ½ cup chopped zucchini
- 1 teaspoon turmeric powder
- ¼ teaspoon black pepper

INSTRUCTIONS

1. In a nonstick pan, warm the olive oil over a medium-high temperature.
2. Cook the onion and green pepper until they become tender.
3. Add crumbled tofu, zucchini, turmeric, and black pepper.
4. Cook, stirring frequently, until heated through and vegetables are tender.

TIPS

- Choose firm or extra-firm tofu for the best texture.
- If desired, you can add a small amount of low-sodium soy sauce for additional flavor.

NUTRITIONAL FACTS

Calories: approximately 200

Protein: 15 grams

Carbohydrates: 8 grams

Fiber: 4 grams

Potassium: 250 milligrams

Phosphorus: 150 milligrams

Sodium: 15 milligrams

PEAR AND GINGER OATMEAL

Yields: one serving | **Prep Time:** 5 minutes | **Cooking Time:** 10 minutes

INGREDIENTS

- ½ cup rolled oats
- 1 cup water
- ½ cup unsweetened rice milk
- ½ pear, diced
- ½ teaspoon ground ginger
- Spices: pinch of cinnamon (optional)

INSTRUCTIONS

1. In a saucepan, combine oats, water, and rice milk.
2. Bring to a boil, then reduce heat and simmer for 5-7 minutes, or until thickened.
3. Stir in diced pear and ginger.
4. Cook for an additional 2-3 minutes, or until pear is softened.
5. Before serving, remove from the heat and allow to cool slightly.

TIPS

- You can add a sprinkle of cinnamon for extra flavor.
- If you prefer a sweeter taste, add a few drops of liquid stevia.
- This oatmeal is a good source of fiber and can help regulate blood sugar levels.

NUTRITIONAL FACTS

Calories: approximately 150

Protein: 5 grams

Carbohydrates: 25 grams

Fiber: 5 grams

Potassium: 200 milligrams

Phosphorus: 75 milligrams

Sodium: 5 milligrams

EGG WHITE SALAD WITH MIXED GREENS AND HERBS

Yields: two servings | **Prep Time:** 15 minutes | **Cooking Time:** 1 minute

INGREDIENTS

- 4 large egg whites
- 1/4 cup finely chopped celery
- 1/4 cup finely chopped red bell pepper
- 1 tablespoon chopped fresh parsley
- 1 tablespoon chopped fresh chives
- 1 tablespoon plain, non-fat Greek yogurt (optional)
- 1 teaspoon Dijon mustard
- 1/2 teaspoon lemon juice
- Black pepper to taste
- 2 cups mixed greens (such as arugula, spinach, or romaine lettuce)

INSTRUCTIONS

1. Hard-boil the egg whites: Place egg whites in a saucepan, cover with cold water, and bring to a boil. Reduce heat to low, cover, and simmer for 1 minute. Remove from heat, let stand for 10 minutes, then drain and cool.
2. Chop egg whites, celery, and red bell pepper into small pieces.
3. In a bowl, combine chopped egg whites, celery, red bell pepper, parsley, chives, Greek yogurt (if using), Dijon mustard, lemon juice, and black pepper.
4. Toss gently to combine.
5. Serve over mixed greens.

TIPS

- This recipe is naturally low in potassium, phosphorus, and sodium.
- If you use Greek yogurt, be sure to choose a plain, non-fat variety to minimize fat and carbohydrate content.
- You can adjust the amount of herbs and spices to your taste.

NUTRITIONAL FACTS

Calories: approximately 100

Protein: ten grams

Carbohydrates: five grams

Fiber: two grams

Potassium: 150 milligrams

Phosphorus: 80 milligrams

Sodium: 50 milligrams (without added salt)

BERRY PARFAIT WITH COCONUT YOGURT

Yields: one serving | **Prep Time:** five minutes

INGREDIENTS

- 1 cup unsweetened frozen berries (strawberries, blueberries, raspberries)
- ½ cup unsweetened coconut yogurt

INSTRUCTIONS

1. In a small bowl or glass, layer frozen berries and coconut yogurt.
2. Repeat layers until all ingredients are used.

TIPS

- Choose unsweetened coconut yogurt to avoid added sugars.
- Frozen berries are a good source of antioxidants and vitamins.
- This parfait is a refreshing and healthy snack or dessert option.

NUTRITIONAL FACTS

Calories: approximately 120

Protein: two grams

Carbohydrates: 15 grams

Fiber: four grams

Potassium: 180 milligrams

Phosphorus: 40 milligrams

Sodium: 10 milligrams

SPINACH AND MUSHROOM OMELET

Yields: one serving | **Prep Time:** 5 minutes | **Cooking Time:** 10 minutes

INGREDIENTS

- 2 large egg whites
- 1 cup fresh spinach, chopped
- 1/4 cup sliced mushrooms
- 1 teaspoon olive oil
- Black pepper to taste

INSTRUCTIONS

1. In a nonstick pan, warm the olive oil over a medium-high temperature.
2. Add chopped spinach and mushrooms, cook until softened.
3. In a bowl, whisk egg whites and black pepper.
4. Pour egg whites into the pan with spinach and mushrooms.
5. Cook, gently lifting the edges to allow uncooked egg to flow underneath, until set.
6. Fold omelet in half and serve immediately.

TIPS

- Use only egg whites to lower cholesterol and phosphorus content.
- Spinach and mushrooms are both excellent sources of nutrients.
- Season with black pepper or other herbs and spices for flavor.

NUTRITIONAL FACTS

Calories: approximately 120

Protein: 10 grams

Carbohydrates: 5 grams

Fiber: 2 grams

Potassium: 160 milligrams

Phosphorus: 80 milligrams

Sodium: 5 milligrams (without added salt)

CAULIFLOWER "OATMEAL" WITH BERRIES AND CINNAMON

Yields: one serving | **Prep Time:** 5 minutes | **Cooking Time:** 10 minutes

INGREDIENTS

- 1 cup riced cauliflower (fresh or frozen)
- 1 cup unsweetened rice milk
- 1/4 cup water
- 1/2 teaspoon vanilla extract
- 1/4 teaspoon ground cinnamon
- 1/2 cup mixed berries (blueberries, raspberries, strawberries)

INSTRUCTIONS

1. In a saucepan, combine riced cauliflower, rice milk, and water.
2. Bring to a boil, then reduce heat and simmer for 5-7 minutes, or until cauliflower is tender.
3. Stir in vanilla extract and cinnamon.
4. Top with mixed berries and serve warm.

TIPS

- This recipe is naturally low in potassium, phosphorus, and sodium.
- Cauliflower is a good source of vitamin C and fiber.
- Berries add sweetness and antioxidants.
- If you prefer a creamier texture, you can blend the cooked cauliflower mixture before adding the berries.

NUTRITIONAL FACTS

Calories: approximately 100

Protein: three grams

Carbohydrates: 15 grams

Fiber: four grams

Potassium: 180 milligrams

Phosphorus: 50 milligrams

Sodium: 10 milligrams

LEMONY ASPARAGUS AND TOFU SCRAMBLE

Yields: two servings | **Prep Time:** 10 minutes | **Cooking Time:** 15 minutes

INGREDIENTS

- 1/2 block firm tofu, drained and crumbled
- 1 tablespoon olive oil
- One bunch of asparagus, thinly sliced into 1-inch segments
- 1/4 cup chopped onion
- 1/4 cup chopped red bell pepper
- 1/2 teaspoon lemon zest
- 1 tablespoon lemon juice
- 1/4 teaspoon black pepper
- Use fresh herbs as garnish, like parsley or chives.

INSTRUCTIONS

1. In a nonstick pan, warm the olive oil over a medium-high temperature.
2. Add onion and bell pepper, cook until softened.
3. Add asparagus and cook until tender-crisp.
4. Add crumbled tofu, lemon zest, lemon juice, and black pepper.
5. Cook, stirring frequently, until heated through.
6. Garnish with fresh herbs and serve.

TIPS

- Choose firm or extra-firm tofu for the best texture.
- Vitamins A, C, and K are all present in abundance in asparagus.
- Lemon zest and juice add a bright, fresh flavor without added sodium.

NUTRITIONAL FACTS

Calories: approximately 200

Protein: 15 grams

Carbohydrates: 8 grams

Fiber: 4 grams

Potassium: 200 milligrams

Phosphorus: 100 milligrams

Sodium: 15 milligrams

BROCCOLI AND EGG WHITE MUFFINS

Yields: 4 muffins | **Prep Time:** 10 minutes | **Cooking Time:** 20-25 minutes

INGREDIENTS

- 1 cup chopped broccoli florets
- 4 large egg whites
- 1/4 cup chopped onion
- 1/4 cup chopped red bell pepper
- 1/4 teaspoon black pepper

INSTRUCTIONS

1. Preheat the oven to 350°F (175°C).
2. Steam or microwave broccoli until tender-crisp.
3. In a bowl, whisk together egg whites and black pepper.
4. Stir in chopped broccoli, onion, and red bell pepper.
5. Divide the mixture evenly among a greased muffin tin.
6. Bake for twenty to twenty-five minutes, until firm and golden brown.

TIPS

- These muffins are a great way to incorporate vegetables into your breakfast or snack.
- You can experiment with different herbs and spices to add flavor.
- Store leftovers in the refrigerator for a quick and easy breakfast option

NUTRITIONAL FACTS

Calories: approximately 50

Protein: 5 grams

Carbohydrates: 3 grams

Fiber: 1 gram

Potassium: 80 milligrams

Phosphorus: 40 milligrams

Sodium: 10 milligrams (without added salt)

SALMON CAKES WITH DILL YOGURT SAUCE

Yields: 4 servings | **Prep Time:** 15 minutes | **Cooking Time:** 10 minutes

INGREDIENTS

- 1 (14.5-ounce) can canned salmon, drained (preferably boneless and skinless)
- 1/4 cup chopped onion
- 1/4 cup chopped celery
- 1 large egg white
- 1 tablespoon flaxseed meal
- 1/4 teaspoon dried dill
- Black pepper to taste

Dill Yogurt Sauce:

- 1/4 cup plain, non-fat Greek yogurt
- One tablespoon of freshly chopped dill (or one teaspoon of dried dill)
- 1 tablespoon lemon juice
- Black pepper to taste

INSTRUCTIONS

1. In a large bowl, combine flaked salmon, onion, celery, egg white, flaxseed meal, dill, and black pepper.
2. Gently fold together to combine.
3. Form the mixture into 4 equal patties.
4. Heat a non-stick skillet over medium heat.
5. Cook salmon cakes for 3-4 minutes per side, or until golden brown and cooked through.
6. Dill Yogurt Sauce:
7. In a small bowl, whisk together yogurt, dill, lemon juice, and black pepper.
8. Serving:
9. Serve salmon cakes with dill yogurt sauce on the side.

TIPS

- Omega-3 fatty acids and protein can be found in abundance in canned salmon.

- Flaxseed meal adds fiber and helps bind the salmon cakes together.

- Dill yogurt sauce is a flavorful and low-sodium topping.

- Be sure to choose canned salmon that is packed in water to avoid added sodium.

NUTRITIONAL FACTS

Calories: approximately 250

Protein: 20 grams

Carbohydrates: 5 grams

Fiber: 2 grams

Potassium: 300 milligrams

Phosphorus: 200 milligrams

Sodium: 70 milligrams (without added salt)

TUNA SALAD WITH CABBAGE WRAPS

Yields: 4 servings | **Prep Time:** 10 minutes

INGREDIENTS

- 6 ounces canned tuna in water, drained
- 2 tablespoons chopped celery
- 1 tablespoon chopped red onion
- 1 tablespoon light mayonnaise (or mashed avocado for a vegan option)
- 1 tablespoon lemon juice
- Black pepper to taste
- 4 large cabbage leaves

INSTRUCTIONS

1. In a bowl, combine flaked tuna, celery, red onion, mayonnaise, lemon juice, and black pepper.
2. Wash and dry cabbage leaves.
3. Spoon tuna salad mixture onto each cabbage leaf.
4. Fold the bottom of the cabbage leaf up over the filling, then roll up from the side.

TIPS

- Canned tuna in water is a good source of lean protein.

- Cabbage leaves are a low-carb and low-calorie alternative to bread.

- Light mayonnaise or mashed avocado adds moisture and flavor without added sodium or potassium.

NUTRITIONAL FACTS

Calories: approximately 150

Protein: 20 grams

Carbohydrates: 5 grams

Fiber: 2 grams

Potassium: 200 milligrams

Phosphorus: 150 milligrams

Sodium: 70 milligrams (without added salt)

CHIA SEED PUDDING WITH BERRIES

Yields: 1 serving | Prep Time: 5 minutes (plus chilling time)

INGREDIENTS

- /4 cup chia seeds
- 1 cup unsweetened almond milk
- 1/4 teaspoon ground cinnamon
- 1/4 teaspoon vanilla extract
- 1/2 cup mixed berries (blueberries, raspberries, strawberries)

INSTRUCTIONS

1. In a bowl or jar, whisk together chia seeds, almond milk, cinnamon, and vanilla extract.
2. Let sit for at least 30 minutes, or overnight, to thicken.
3. Top with mixed berries before serving.

TIPS

- Omega-3 fatty acids and fiber are abundant in chia seeds.
- Almond milk is naturally low in potassium and phosphorus.
- This recipe is a quick and easy breakfast or snack option that provides healthy fats and fiber.

NUTRITIONAL FACTS

Calories: approximately 200

Protein: 4 grams

Carbohydrates: 15 grams

Fiber: 8 grams

Potassium: 100 milligrams

Phosphorus: 80 milligrams

Sodium: 10 milligrams

OATMEAL WITH PEAR AND SPICES

Yields: 1 serving | **Prep Time:** 5 minutes | **Cooking Time:** 8-10 minutes

INGREDIENTS

- 1/2 cup rolled oats
- 1 cup water
- 1/2 cup unsweetened rice milk (or almond milk)
- 1/2 pear, diced
- 1/4 teaspoon ground ginger
- 1/4 teaspoon ground cinnamon

INSTRUCTIONS

1. In a saucepan, combine oats and water.
2. After bringing to a boil, lower heat, and simmer for five minutes.
3. Stir in rice milk (or almond milk), diced pear, ginger, and cinnamon.
4. Continue simmering for another 2-3 minutes, or until the oatmeal reaches desired consistency.
5. When ready to serve, remove from heat and allow it cool slightly.

TIPS

- Oatmeal is a good source of soluble fiber, which can help lower cholesterol and regulate blood sugar levels.
- Choose unsweetened rice milk or almond milk to avoid added sugars.
- Pears are a low-potassium fruit option that adds sweetness and fiber.
- The amount of spices can be changed to suit your preferences.
- If desired, you can top the oatmeal with a sprinkle of chopped nuts (in moderation, but if you are on extremely low potassium skip nuts totally) for added protein and healthy fats.

NUTRITIONAL FACTS

Calories: 150 (approx.)

Fat: 10g (approx.)

Carbohydrates: 15g (approx.)

Protein: 2g (approx.)

Sodium: (to be determined based on salt used)

CHAPTER 4

LUNCH RECIPES

CHICKEN SALAD LETTUCE WRAPS WITH LEMON-DILL DRESSING

Yields: 4 servings | **Prep Time:** 15 minutes

INGREDIENTS

- 1 cup cooked, shredded chicken breast (skinless)
- 1/4 cup finely chopped celery
- 1/4 cup finely chopped red onion
- 1 tablespoon chopped fresh dill
- 1/4 cup plain, non-fat Greek yogurt
- 1 tablespoon lemon juice
- 1/4 teaspoon black pepper
- Four big leaves of lettuce (romaine or butter lettuce)

INSTRUCTIONS

1. In a medium bowl, combine shredded chicken, celery, red onion, and dill.
2. In a separate small bowl, whisk together Greek yogurt, lemon juice, and black pepper to make the dressing.
3. Mix the chicken mixture with the dressing after pouring it over it.
4. Divide chicken salad evenly among lettuce leaves. Roll up and enjoy!

TIPS

- This recipe is a good source of lean protein and low in carbohydrates.

- Using Greek yogurt instead of mayonnaise reduces fat and calories.

- Select lettuce leaves that are big enough and strong enough to support the filling.

- If desired, you can add a sprinkle of paprika or other herbs for extra flavor.

NUTRITIONAL FACTS

Calories: approximately 150

Protein: 20 grams

Carbohydrates: 5 grams

Fiber: 2 grams

Potassium: 250 milligrams

Phosphorus: 180 milligrams

Sodium: 50 milligrams

SALMON WITH ROASTED CAULIFLOWER AND LEMON-DILL SAUCE

Yields: 4 servings | **Prep Time:** 10 minutes | **Cooking Time:** 30-35 minutes

INGREDIENTS

- 4 (4-ounce) salmon fillets
- 1 head cauliflower, cut into florets
- 1 tablespoon olive oil
- 1/4 teaspoon black pepper
- Lemon-Dill Sauce
- 1/4 cup plain, non-fat Greek yogurt
- One tablespoon of freshly chopped dill (or one teaspoon of dried dill)
- 1 tablespoon lemon juice
- 1/4 teaspoon black pepper

INSTRUCTIONS

1. Preheat oven to 400°F (200°C).
2. Toss cauliflower florets with olive oil and black pepper. Arrange in a solitary layer upon a baking tray.
3. Roast cauliflower for 20-25 minutes, or until tender and slightly browned.
4. Meanwhile, prepare lemon-dill sauce by whisking together yogurt, dill, lemon juice, and black pepper in a small bowl.
5. Salmon fillets should be put on a different baking sheet.
6. Bake salmon for 12-15 minutes, or until cooked through.
7. Serve salmon with roasted cauliflower and a drizzle of lemon-dill sauce.

TIPS

- Omega-3 fatty acids are great for heart health and are found in abundance in salmon.
- Roasting cauliflower brings out its natural sweetness and caramelizes the edges.
- The lemon-dill sauce adds a bright and refreshing flavor without adding sodium.

NUTRITIONAL FACTS

Calories: approximately 300

Protein: 30 grams

Carbohydrates: 10 grams

Fiber: 4 grams

Potassium: 450 milligrams

Phosphorus: 350 milligrams

Sodium: 100 milligrams

LEMONY CHICKEN SOUP WITH HERBS

Yields: 4 servings | **Prep Time:** 10 minutes | **Cooking Time:** 20 minutes

INGREDIENTS

- 4 cups low-sodium chicken broth
- 1 cup cooked, shredded chicken breast (skinless)
- 1/2 cup chopped carrots
- 1/2 cup chopped celery
- 1/4 cup chopped onion
- 1/4 cup chopped fresh parsley
- 1/4 cup chopped fresh dill
- 1 tablespoon lemon juice
- 1/4 teaspoon black pepper

INSTRUCTIONS

1. In a large pot, combine chicken broth, shredded chicken, carrots, celery, and onion.
2. After bringing to a boil, lower the heat, and simmer for fifteen minutes.
3. Stir in parsley, dill, lemon juice, and black pepper.
4. Simmer for an additional 5 minutes, or until vegetables are tender.

TIPS

- To cut back on sodium, use low-sodium chicken broth.

- This soup is a good source of lean protein and vegetables.

- Fresh herbs add flavor and nutrients without adding sodium.

- If desired, you can add a small amount of cooked rice or quinoa to the soup for additional carbohydrates and fiber.

NUTRITIONAL FACTS

Calories: approximately 150

Protein: 15 grams

Carbohydrates: 5 grams

Fiber: 2 grams

Potassium: 200 milligrams

Phosphorus: 100 milligrams

Sodium: 150 milligrams (depending on the sodium content of the broth)

TUNA SALAD WITH CELERY AND GRAPES ON LETTUCE

Yields: 4 servings | **Prep time:** 10 minutes | **Serving Size: 1** lettuce wrap

INGREDIENTS

- 5 ounces can tuna in water, drained
- 1/4 cup finely chopped celery
- 1/4 cup halved red grapes
- 2 tablespoons plain, non-fat Greek yogurt
- 1 teaspoon Dijon mustard
- 1/2 teaspoon lemon juice
- Black pepper to taste
- Four big leaves of lettuce (romaine or butter lettuce)

INSTRUCTIONS

1. In a medium bowl, combine tuna, celery, grapes, yogurt, mustard, lemon juice, and black pepper.
2. Gently toss to combine.
3. Divide tuna salad evenly among lettuce leaves, spooning it into the center.
4. Fold or roll up the lettuce leaves to enclose the tuna salad.

TIPS

- Opt for tuna packed in water to avoid added sodium.
- Plain, non-fat Greek yogurt is a healthier alternative to mayonnaise, providing protein and probiotics.
- Grapes add natural sweetness and a bit of extra fiber.
- Use fresh dill for optimal flavor.
- You can adjust the amount of ingredients to your preference.

NUTRITIONAL FACTS

Calories: 100

Protein: 15 grams

Carbohydrates: 3 grams

Fiber: 1 gram

Potassium: 150 milligrams

Phosphorus: 100 milligrams

Sodium: 45 milligrams

TUNA SALAD WITH CELERY AND GRAPES ON LETTUCE

Yields: 4 servings | **Prep time:** 10 minutes | **Serving Size:** 1 lettuce wrap

INGREDIENTS

- 2 ripe avocados, pitted and diced
- 1 cup cooked, shredded chicken breast (skinless)
- 1 cup riced cauliflower (fresh or frozen)
- 1/2 cup chopped broccoli florets
- 1/2 cup chopped carrots
- 1/4 cup chopped green bell pepper
- 1 tablespoon olive oil
- 1/4 cup low-sodium chicken broth
- 1/2 teaspoon garlic powder
- 1/4 teaspoon onion powder
- 1/4 teaspoon dried thyme
- 1/4 teaspoon black pepper

INSTRUCTIONS

1. In a big wok or skillet, warm up the olive oil over a medium-high temperature.
2. Add onion, broccoli, and carrots, and stir-fry for 3-4 minutes, or until tender-crisp.
3. Add riced cauliflower and cook for 2-3 minutes, or until heated through.
4. Stir in shredded chicken, broth, and spices.
5. Cook for a further two to three minutes, or until well heated.

TIPS

- This recipe is a good source of lean protein and fiber.
- Cauliflower rice is a low-carb alternative to white rice.
- To cut back on sodium, use low-sodium chicken broth.
- Add other low-potassium vegetables, such as zucchini or green beans.

NUTRITIONAL FACTS

Calories: 200

Protein: 20 grams

Carbohydrates: 8 grams

Fiber: 3 grams

Potassium: 280 milligrams

Phosphorus: 150 milligrams

Sodium: 100 milligrams (depending on the sodium content of chicken broth)

CUCUMBER AND BELL PEPPER SALAD WITH LEMON-HERB VINAIGRETTE

Yields: 4 servings | **Prep Time:** 10 minutes | **Serving Size:** 1 cup

INGREDIENTS

- 1 cucumber, thinly sliced
- 1 bell pepper (any color), thinly sliced
- 1/4 cup finely chopped fresh herbs (parsley, dill, or chives)

Lemon-Herb Vinaigrette:

- 1 tablespoon olive oil
- 2 tablespoons lemon juice
- 1/2 teaspoon Dijon mustard
- 1/4 teaspoon black pepper

INSTRUCTIONS

1. In a separate small bowl, whisk together olive oil, lemon juice, mustard, and black pepper to make the vinaigrette.
2. Drizzle the salad with the dressing and mix to coat.

TIPS

- This salad is a refreshing and hydrating side dish or light lunch option.
- It is naturally low in potassium, phosphorus, and sodium.
- The lemon-herb vinaigrette adds a bright and flavorful touch without adding extra sodium.
- You can adjust the amount of herbs and vegetables to your liking.

NUTRITIONAL FACTS

Calories: 50

Protein: 1 gram

Carbohydrates: 4 grams

Fiber: 2 grams

Potassium: 150 milligrams

Phosphorus: 20 milligrams

Sodium: 5 milligrams

QUINOA SALAD WITH BLACK BEANS AND LEMON VINAIGRETTE

Yields: 2 servings | **Prep Time:** 15 minutes | **Cooking Time:** 15-20 minutes (for cooking quinoa) | **Serving Size:** 1 1/2 cups

INGREDIENTS

- 1/2 cup quinoa, cooked
- Half a cup of washed and drained canned black beans
- 1/4 cup chopped red onion
- 1/4 cup chopped cucumber
- 1/4 cup chopped green bell pepper
- 1/4 cup chopped fresh cilantro
- Lemon Vinaigrette:
- 1 tablespoon olive oil
- 2 tablespoons lemon juice
- 1/2 teaspoon Dijon mustard
- Black pepper to taste

INSTRUCTIONS

1. In a large bowl, combine cooked quinoa, black beans, red onion, cucumber, bell pepper, and cilantro.
2. In a separate small bowl, whisk together olive oil, lemon juice, mustard, and black pepper to make the vinaigrette.
3. Drizzle the salad with the dressing and mix to combine

TIPS

- Quinoa is a good source of protein and fiber, making it a satisfying and nutritious base for this salad.
- Black beans add additional protein and fiber while being low in potassium.
- The lemon vinaigrette adds flavor without extra sodium.
- If you are sensitive to FODMAPs, you may want to omit the onion and garlic.

NUTRITIONAL FACTS

Calories: 250

Protein: 10 grams

Carbohydrates: 30 grams

Fiber: 6 grams

Potassium: 280 milligrams

Phosphorus: 150 milligrams

Sodium: 30 milligrams

TURKEY LETTUCE WRAPS WITH SPICY YOGURT SAUCE

Yields: 4 servings | **Prep Time:** 10 minutes | **Cooking Time:** 15 minutes | **Serving Size:** 1 lettuce wrap

INGREDIENTS

- 1/2 pound ground turkey
- 1/4 cup chopped onion
- 1/4 cup chopped green bell pepper
- 1/4 teaspoon garlic powder
- 1/4 teaspoon onion powder
- 1/4 teaspoon chili powder
- 1/4 teaspoon cumin
- Black pepper to taste
- Four big leaves of lettuce (romaine or butter lettuce)

Spicy Yogurt Sauce:

- 1/4 cup plain, non-fat Greek yogurt
- 1/4 teaspoon sriracha sauce (or to taste)
- 1/4 teaspoon lime juice

INSTRUCTIONS

5. In a medium bowl, combine diced avocado, tomatillos, jalapeño, red onion, cilantro, lime juice, sea salt, and black pepper.
6. Gently stir to combine all ingredients.
7. Taste and adjust seasonings as desired.

TIPS

- Ground turkey is a lean protein source that is lower in phosphorus than red meat.
- Lettuce wraps are a low-carb alternative to tortillas or bread.
- The spicy yogurt sauce adds a flavorful kick without adding sodium.
- If you are sensitive to spicy foods, you can reduce or omit the sriracha sauce.

NUTRITIONAL FACTS

Calories: 150

Protein: 20 grams

Carbohydrates: 5 grams

Fiber: 2 grams

Potassium: 200 milligrams

Phosphorus: 150 milligrams

Sodium: 50 milligrams

ZUCCHINI NOODLES WITH PESTO AND GRILLED CHICKEN

Yields: 2 servings | **Prep Time:** 10 minutes | **Cooking Time:** 5 minutes | **Serving Size:** 1 1/2 cups

INGREDIENTS

- 2 medium zucchini, spiralized into noodles
- 1/2 cup cooked, shredded chicken breast (skinless)
- 1/4 cup pesto (homemade or store-bought, check for low-sodium options)

INSTRUCTIONS

1. Heat a non-stick skillet over medium heat.
2. Add zucchini noodles and cook for 2-3 minutes, or until tender-crisp.
3. Stir in shredded chicken and pesto.
4. Heat through and serve immediately.

TIPS

- Zucchini noodles are a low-carb and low-potassium alternative to pasta.
- Chicken provides lean protein.
- Pesto adds flavor and healthy fats.
- Be sure to choose a low-sodium pesto or make your own to control sodium intake.
- To create zucchini ribbons without a spiralizer, use a vegetable peeler.

NUTRITIONAL FACTS

Calories: 200

Protein: 20 grams

Carbohydrates: 8 grams

Fiber: 3 grams

Potassium: 250 milligrams

Phosphorus: 100 milligrams

Sodium: 100 milligrams (depending on the sodium content of pesto)

CAULIFLOWER RICE BOWL WITH SHRIMP AND VEGETABLES

Yields: 2 servings | **Prep Time:** 10 minutes | **Cooking Time:** 10-12 minutes | **Serving Size:** 1 cup

INGREDIENTS

- 1 cup riced cauliflower (fresh or frozen)
- 1/2 cup cooked shrimp
- 1/4 cup chopped broccoli florets
- 1/4 cup chopped carrots
- 1/4 cup chopped green beans
- 1 tablespoon olive oil
- 1/4 cup low-sodium chicken broth
- 1/4 teaspoon garlic powder
- 1/4 teaspoon onion powder
- Pinch of red pepper flakes (optional)
- Fresh herbs (such as parsley or chives) for garnish

INSTRUCTIONS

1. Warm up the olive oil in a skillet over a medium temperature.
2. Add broccoli, carrots, and green beans. Stir-fry for 3-4 minutes, or until tender-crisp.
3. Add riced cauliflower and cook for 2-3 minutes, or until heated through.
4. Stir in shrimp, chicken broth, garlic powder, onion powder, and red pepper flakes (if using).
5. Cook for an additional 2-3 minutes, or until shrimp is heated through.
6. Garnish with fresh herbs and serve.

TIPS

- This recipe is a good source of lean protein and vegetables.

- Cauliflower rice is a low-carb and low-potassium alternative to traditional rice.

- Both protein and omega-3 fatty acids are found in abundance in prawns.

- Use low-sodium chicken broth to reduce sodium intake.

- Feel free to substitute other low-potassium vegetables like zucchini or asparagus.

NUTRITIONAL FACTS

Calories: 200

Protein: 18 grams

Carbohydrates: 10 grams

Fiber: 4 grams

Potassium: 250 milligrams

Phosphorus: 120 milligrams

Sodium: 100 milligrams (depending on the sodium content of the broth)

SPINACH SALAD WITH GRILLED CHICKEN AND BALSAMIC VINAIGRETTE

Yields: 2 servings | **Prep Time:** 10 minutes | **Cooking Time:** (Grilling time for chicken not included) | **Serving Size:** 1 cup

INGREDIENTS

- 2 cups fresh baby spinach
- 4 ounces grilled chicken breast, sliced
- 1/4 cup sliced cucumber
- 1/4 cup sliced red onion
- Balsamic Vinaigrette:
- 1 tablespoon olive oil
- 1 tablespoon balsamic vinegar
- 1/2 teaspoon Dijon mustard
- Black pepper to taste

INSTRUCTIONS

1. In a large bowl, combine spinach, grilled chicken, cucumber, and red onion.
2. In a separate small bowl, whisk together olive oil, balsamic vinegar, mustard, and black pepper to make the vinaigrette.
3. Drizzle the salad with the dressing and mix to combine.

TIPS

- This salad is a healthy and satisfying meal option that is low in carbohydrates and calories.
- Spinach is a good source of iron and vitamin K.
- Grilled chicken provides lean protein.
- Balsamic vinegar adds a tangy flavor without the need for added salt.

NUTRITIONAL FACTS

Calories: 200

Protein: 20 grams

Carbohydrates: 5 grams

Fiber: 2 grams

Potassium: 200 milligrams

Phosphorus: 150 milligrams

Sodium: 50 milligrams

LEMONY CHICKPEA SALAD WITH FRESH HERBS

Yields: 4 servings | **Prep Time:** 10 minutes | **Serving Size:** 1/2 cup

INGREDIENTS

- 1 (15-ounce) can chickpeas, rinsed and drained
- 1/4 cup chopped red onion
- 1/4 cup chopped cucumber
- 1/4 cup chopped fresh parsley
- 1/4 cup chopped fresh mint
- 2 tablespoons lemon juice
- 1 tablespoon olive oil
- Black pepper to taste

INSTRUCTIONS

1. In a medium bowl, combine chickpeas, red onion, cucumber, parsley, and mint.
2. In a separate small bowl, whisk together lemon juice, olive oil, and black pepper.
3. Drizzle the chickpea mixture with the dressing and shake to distribute the dressing.

TIPS

-
- Chickpeas are an excellent source of fiber and protein.
- This salad is a refreshing and healthy option that can be served as a side dish or light lunch.
- Lemon juice and fresh herbs add flavor without the need for salt.
- You can use this salad as a sandwich filling or lettuce wrap filling.

Calories: 200

Protein: 10 grams

Carbohydrates: 20 grams

Fiber: 6 grams

Potassium: 250 milligrams

Phosphorus: 100 milligrams

Sodium: 10 milligrams

BAKED FISH TACOS WITH CABBAGE SLAW

Yields: 4 servings | **Prep Time:** 10 minutes | **Cooking Time:** 20 minutes | **Serving Size:** 1 cup

INGREDIENTS

- 4 cups low-sodium chicken broth
- 1 cup chopped broccoli florets
- 1/2 cup cooked, shredded chicken breast (skinless)
- 1/4 cup chopped onion
- 1/4 cup chopped carrots
- 1/4 teaspoon garlic powder
- 1/4 teaspoon onion powder
- 1/4 teaspoon dried thyme
- Black pepper to taste

INSTRUCTIONS

1. In a large pot, combine chicken broth, broccoli, chicken, onion, and carrots.
2. Bring to a boil, then reduce heat and simmer for 10-15 minutes, or until vegetables are tender.
3. Stir in garlic powder, onion powder, thyme, and black pepper.
4. Simmer for an additional 5 minutes.

TIPS

- To limit your intake of sodium, use low-sodium chicken broth.

- Broccoli and carrots are good sources of vitamins and fiber.

- Chicken provides lean protein.

- This soup is a warm and comforting meal that is easy to digest.

NUTRITIONAL FACTS

Calories: 150

Protein: 15 grams

Carbohydrates: 8 grams

Fiber: 4 grams

Potassium: 200 milligrams

Phosphorus: 100 milligrams

Sodium: 100 milligrams (depending on the sodium content of the broth)

VEGGIE BURGER ON A LETTUCE BUN WITH MUSTARD

Yields: 1 serving | **Prep Time:** 5 minutes | **Cooking Time:** 10-15 minutes (depending on the veggie burger) | **Serving Size:** 1 burger

INGREDIENTS

- 1 veggie burger (check the ingredients to ensure it's low in sodium, potassium, and phosphorus)
- 2 large lettuce leaves (butter lettuce or romaine)
- 1 tablespoon Dijon mustard

INSTRUCTIONS

1. Cook veggie burger according to package directions.
2. Spread mustard on lettuce leaves.
3. Place cooked veggie burger on lettuce leaves.

TIPS

- Choose a veggie burger that is made with whole food ingredients and is low in sodium, potassium, and phosphorus.
- Lettuce leaves are a low-carb and low-potassium alternative to bread.
- Mustard adds flavor without adding sodium.
- If desired, you can add other low-potassium vegetables, such as sliced cucumber or onion, to the burger.

NUTRITIONAL FACTS

Calories: 200-300 (depending on the veggie burger)

Protein: 10-15 grams

Carbohydrates: 10-20 grams

Fiber: 5-10 grams

Potassium: 200-300 milligrams

Phosphorus: 100-150 milligrams

Sodium: 100-200 milligrams (depending on the veggie burger)

CHAPTER 5

DINNER RECIPES

BAKED CHICKEN WITH ROSEMARY AND ROASTED VEGETABLES

Yields: 2 servings | **Prep Time:** 10 minutes | **Cooking Time:** 30 minutes | **Serving Size:** 1 chicken breast + 1 cup vegetables

INGREDIENTS

- 2 boneless, skinless chicken breasts
- 1 tablespoon olive oil
- 1 teaspoon dried rosemary
- 1/4 teaspoon black pepper
- 1 cup broccoli florets
- 1 cup cauliflower florets
- Half a cup of green beans, cleaned and sliced into one-inch pieces

INSTRUCTIONS

1. Preheat oven to 400°F (200°C).
2. In a small bowl, combine olive oil, rosemary, and black pepper.
3. Rub the mixture onto the chicken breasts.
4. Place chicken breasts in a baking dish.
5. In a separate bowl, toss broccoli, cauliflower, and green beans with a drizzle of olive oil and black pepper.

6. Spread vegetables around the chicken in the baking dish.

7. Bake for 25-30 minutes, or until chicken is cooked through and vegetables are tender

TIPS

- Lean protein can be found in chicken breast.
- Use fresh rosemary for the best flavor.
- Broccoli, cauliflower, and green beans are low in potassium and high in fiber.
- To reduce potassium further, you can parboil the vegetables before roasting.

NUTRITIONAL FACTS

Calories: 250

Protein: 30 grams

Carbohydrates: 5 grams

Fiber: 4 grams

Potassium: 400 milligrams

Phosphorus: 200 milligrams

Sodium: 50 milligrams

SALMON WITH LEMON-DILL SAUCE AND ASPARAGUS

Yields: 2 servings | **Prep Time:** 10 minutes | **Cooking Time:** 15 minutes | **Serving Size:** 1 salmon fillet + 1/4 pound asparagus

INGREDIENTS

- 2 (4-ounce) salmon fillets
- 1 tablespoon olive oil
- 1/4 teaspoon black pepper
- 1/2 pound asparagus spears, trimmed
- Lemon-Dill Sauce:
- 1/4 cup plain, non-fat Greek yogurt
- 1 tablespoon chopped fresh dill (or 1 teaspoon dried dill)
- 1 tablespoon lemon juice
- Black pepper to taste

INSTRUCTIONS

1. Preheat oven to 400°F (200°C).
2. Arrange the salmon fillets on a parchment paper-lined baking pan.
3. Add a drizzle of olive oil and a pinch of black pepper.
4. Place asparagus spears on a separate baking sheet.
5. Add a drizzle of olive oil and a pinch of black pepper.
6. Bake salmon for 12-15 minutes, or until cooked through.
7. Bake asparagus for 10-12 minutes, or until tender-crisp.
8. While the salmon and asparagus are baking, prepare the lemon-dill sauce by whisking together yogurt, dill, lemon juice, and black pepper in a small bowl.

9. Serve salmon and asparagus with a drizzle of lemon-dill sauce.

TIPS

- Heart health benefits from the abundance of omega-3 fatty acids found in salmon.
- Asparagus is a low-calorie, low-carb vegetable that is high in fiber and vitamins.
- The lemon-dill sauce adds flavor without adding salt.

NUTRITIONAL FACTS

Calories: 300

Protein: 30 grams

Carbohydrates: 5 grams

Fiber: 2 grams

Potassium: 400 milligrams

Phosphorus: 300 milligrams

Sodium: 75 milligrams

TURKEY CHILI WITH ZUCCHINI AND SPICES

Yields: 4 servings | **Prep Time:** 15 minutes | **Cooking Time:** 30 minutes | **Serving Size:** 1 cup

INGREDIENTS

- 1 pound ground turkey
- 1 tablespoon olive oil
- 1 onion, chopped
- 2 cloves garlic, minced
- 2 zucchini, diced
- One fifteen-ounce can of washed and drained low-sodium kidney beans
- 1 cup low-sodium chicken broth
- 1 tablespoon chili powder
- 1 teaspoon cumin
- 1/2 teaspoon oregano
- 1/4 teaspoon black pepper

INSTRUCTIONS

1. In a big pot, warm up the olive oil over a medium-high temperature.
2. Add ground turkey and cook until browned, breaking it up with a spoon.
3. Add onion and garlic, and cook until softened.
4. Stir in zucchini, kidney beans, chicken broth, chili powder, cumin, oregano, and black pepper.
5. Bring to a boil, then reduce heat and simmer for 20-25 minutes, or until zucchini is tender.

TIPS

- Ground turkey is a lean source of protein.

- Zucchini adds volume and fiber to the chili.

- Kidney beans are a good source of plant-based protein and fiber.

- Use low-sodium chicken broth to reduce sodium intake.

- This chili can be served with a dollop of plain, non-fat Greek yogurt for added protein and creaminess

NUTRITIONAL FACTS

Calories: 300

Protein: 25 grams

Carbohydrates: 15 grams

Fiber: 7 grams

Potassium: 350 milligrams

Phosphorus: 250 milligrams

Sodium: 100 milligrams (depending on the sodium content of the broth)

SHRIMP SCAMPI WITH ZUCCHINI NOODLES

Yields: 4 servings | **Prep Time:** 10 minutes | **Cooking Time:** 10 minutes | **Serving Size:** 1 cup

INGREDIENTS

- 1 pound large shrimp, peeled and deveined
- 2 medium zucchini, spiralized into noodles
- 2 cloves garlic, minced
- 1 tablespoon olive oil
- 1/4 cup low-sodium chicken broth
- 1 tablespoon lemon juice
- 1/4 teaspoon red pepper flakes
- 1/4 cup chopped fresh parsley

INSTRUCTIONS

1. Sauté the garlic for 30 seconds, or until it becomes aromatic.
2. Add garlic and cook for 30 seconds, or until fragrant.
3. Add shrimp and cook for 2-3 minutes per side, or until pink and cooked through.
4. Remove shrimp from pan and set aside.
5. Add zucchini noodles to the skillet and cook for 2-3 minutes, or until tender-crisp.
6. Stir in chicken broth, lemon juice, and red pepper flakes.
7. Return shrimp to the skillet and cook for 1 minute more, or until heated through.
8. Stir in parsley and serve immediately.

TIPS

- Omega-3 fatty acids and lean protein are both abundant in prawns.
- Zucchini noodles are a low-carb and low-potassium alternative to pasta.
- Use low-sodium chicken broth to reduce sodium intake.
- Garnish with additional herbs like dill or basil for extra flavor.

NUTRITIONAL FACTS

Calories: 200

Protein: 25 grams

Carbohydrates: 8 grams

Fiber: 2 grams

Potassium: 250 milligrams

Phosphorus: 200 milligrams

Sodium: 100 milligrams

CHICKEN AND VEGETABLE CURRY WITH CAULIFLOWER RICE

Yields: 4 servings | **Prep Time:** 15 minutes | **Cooking Time:** 30 minutes | **Serving Size:** 1 cup

INGREDIENTS

- One-pound chicken breasts, skinless and boneless, sliced into 1-inch pieces
- 1 tablespoon olive oil
- 1 onion, chopped
- 2 cloves garlic, minced
- 1 cup cauliflower rice
- 1 cup broccoli florets
- Half a cup of green beans, cleaned and sliced into one-inch pieces
- 1 (14 ounce) can full-fat coconut milk
- 2 tablespoons mild curry powder
- 1/2 teaspoon ground turmeric
- 1/4 teaspoon black pepper

INSTRUCTIONS

1. Cook the chicken until it turns golden brown on all sides.
2. Add onion and garlic, and cook until softened.
3. Stir in cauliflower rice, broccoli, green beans, coconut milk, curry powder, turmeric, and black pepper.
4. Bring to a simmer, then reduce heat and cook for 15-20 minutes, or until vegetables are tender and sauce has thickened.

TIPS

- Lean protein can be found in abundance in chicken.
- Cauliflower rice is a low-carb and low-potassium alternative to white rice.
- Full-fat coconut milk adds richness and creaminess without adding sugar.
- Use mild curry powder to avoid excess sodium.

NUTRITIONAL FACTS

Calories: 350

Protein: 30 grams

Carbohydrates: 15 grams

Fiber: 5 grams

Potassium: 400 milligrams

Phosphorus: 250 milligrams

Sodium: 100 milligrams

BAKED COD WITH LEMON AND HERBS

Yields: 4 servings | **Prep Time:** 5 minutes | **Cooking Time:** 15 minutes | **Serving Size:** 1 fillet

INGREDIENTS

- 4 (4-ounce) cod fillets
- 1 tablespoon olive oil
- 1 lemon, thinly sliced
- 1/4 cup chopped fresh herbs (such as parsley, dill, and thyme)
- Black pepper to taste

INSTRUCTIONS

1. Preheat oven to 400°F (200°C).
2. Cod fillets should be placed on a parchment paper-lined baking pan.
3. Add a little olive oil and black pepper for seasoning.
4. Top each fillet with lemon slices and sprinkle with fresh herbs.
5. Fish should flake easily with a fork and be cooked through after Twelve to fifteen minutes of baking in the oven.

TIPS

- Cod is a lean and mild-flavored fish that is low in mercury.
- Lemon and herbs add flavor without the need for salt.
- Baking is a healthy cooking method that does not require added fat.
- If you prefer a crispier skin, you can broil the fish for the last few minutes of cooking.

NUTRITIONAL FACTS

Calories: 150

Protein: 20 grams

Carbohydrates: 2 grams

Fiber: 0 grams

Potassium: 200 milligrams

Phosphorus: 200 milligrams

Sodium: 50 milligrams

TOFU STIR-FRY WITH VEGETABLES AND CAULIFLOWER RICE

Yields: 4 servings | **Prep Time:** 15 minutes | **Cooking Time:** 15 minutes | **Serving Size:** 1 cup

INGREDIENTS

- Fourteen ounces of firm or extra-firm tofu, drained and pressed
- 1 tablespoon olive oil
- 1/2 cup chopped onion
- 1/2 cup chopped green bell pepper
- 1/2 cup chopped broccoli florets
- 1/2 cup chopped zucchini
- 1 clove garlic, minced
- 1/2 teaspoon ground ginger
- 1/4 teaspoon turmeric
- Black pepper to taste
- 1 cup riced cauliflower (fresh or frozen)
- 2 tablespoons low-sodium soy sauce (or tamari for gluten-free)

INSTRUCTIONS

1. Cut tofu into 1-inch cubes.
2. On moderately high heat, warm up the olive oil in a big skillet or wok.
3. Cook until tofu is golden brown on all sides after adding it.
4. Add onion, bell pepper, broccoli, and zucchini. Stir-fry for 3-4 minutes, or until tender-crisp.
5. Add garlic, ginger, turmeric, and black pepper. Stir-fry for 1 minute more.
6. Stir in cauliflower rice and soy sauce. Cook for 2-3 minutes, or until heated through.

TIPS

- Tofu is a good source of plant-based protein and low in potassium.

- Cauliflower rice is a low-carb and low-potassium alternative to white rice.

- Use low-sodium soy sauce to reduce sodium intake.

- Be sure to press the tofu to remove excess moisture for better browning.

NUTRITIONAL FACTS

Calories: 250

Protein: 18 grams

Carbohydrates: 12 grams

Fiber: 4 grams

Potassium: 350 milligrams

Phosphorus: 180 milligrams

Sodium: 100 milligrams (depending on the sodium content of soy sauce)

ROASTED CHICKEN WITH LEMON HERBS AND ROASTED VEGETABLES

Yields: 2 servings | **Prep Time:** 10 minutes | **Cooking Time:** 30 minutes | **Serving Size:** 1 chicken breast + 1 cup vegetables

INGREDIENTS

- 2 boneless, skinless chicken breasts
- 1 tablespoon olive oil
- 1 teaspoon dried rosemary
- 1/2 teaspoon dried thyme
- 1/4 teaspoon black pepper
- 1/2 lemon, thinly sliced
- 1 cup broccoli florets
- 1 cup cauliflower florets

INSTRUCTIONS

1. Preheat oven to 400°F (200°C).
2. In a small bowl, combine olive oil, rosemary, thyme, and black pepper.
3. Rub the mixture over the chicken breasts.
4. Place chicken breasts in a baking dish and top with lemon slices.
5. In a separate bowl, toss broccoli and cauliflower with a drizzle of olive oil and black pepper.
6. Spread vegetables around the chicken in the baking dish.
7. Bake for 25-30 minutes, or until chicken is cooked through and vegetables are tender.

TIPS

- Lean protein can be found in chicken breasts.
- Use fresh herbs for the best flavor.
- Broccoli and cauliflower are low in potassium and high in fiber.

NUTRITIONAL FACTS

Calories: 250

Protein: 30 grams

Carbohydrates: 5 grams

Fiber: 4 grams

Potassium: 350 milligrams

Phosphorus: 200 milligrams

Sodium: 50 milligrams

ONE-PAN BAKED SALMON WITH ASPARAGUS AND ZUCCHINI

Yields: 2 servings | **Prep Time:** 10 minutes | **Cooking Time:** 15 minutes | **Serving Size:** 1 salmon fillet + 1/2 of the vegetables

INGREDIENTS

- 2 (4-ounce) salmon fillets
- 1 bunch asparagus, trimmed
- 1 medium zucchini, thinly sliced
- 1 tablespoon olive oil
- 1/2 lemon, thinly sliced
- 1/4 teaspoon black pepper

INSTRUCTIONS

1. Preheat oven to 400°F (200°C).
2. In a baking dish, arrange asparagus and zucchini in a single layer.
3. Add a little olive oil and black pepper for seasoning.
4. Place salmon fillets on top of the vegetables. Top each fillet with lemon slices.
5. Bake for 12-15 minutes, or until salmon is cooked through and vegetables are tender.

TIPS

- Omega-3 fatty acids, which are good for the heart, are abundant in salmon.
- Asparagus and zucchini are low-calorie, low-carb vegetables that are high in fiber and vitamins.
- Lemon adds flavor without the need for salt.

NUTRITIONAL FACTS

Calories: 300

Protein: 30 grams

Carbohydrates: 8 grams

Fiber: 3 grams

Potassium: 350 milligrams

Phosphorus: 280 milligrams

Sodium: 50 milligrams

GRILLED CHICKEN SALAD WITH LEMON-HERB VINAIGRETTE

Yields: 2 servings | **Prep Time**: 10 minutes | **Cooking Time**: 10-14 minutes | **Serving Size**: 1 cup

INGREDIENTS

- 4 ounces boneless, skinless chicken breast
- 1 tablespoon olive oil
- 1/4 teaspoon dried thyme
- 1/4 teaspoon black pepper
- 2 cups mixed greens (such as arugula, spinach, or romaine lettuce)
- 1/4 cup chopped cucumber
- 1/4 cup chopped red bell pepper
- One tablespoon of finely chopped fresh herbs, like chives, dill, or parsley

Lemon-Herb Vinaigrette:

- 2 tablespoons olive oil
- 2 tablespoons lemon juice
- 1/2 teaspoon Dijon mustard
- 1/4 teaspoon dried thyme
- Black pepper to taste

INSTRUCTIONS

1. Rub chicken breast with olive oil, thyme, and black pepper.
2. Grill chicken over medium heat for 5-7 minutes per side, or until cooked through.
3. While chicken is cooking, combine mixed greens, cucumber, bell pepper, and fresh herbs in a large bowl.
4. In a separate small bowl, whisk together olive oil, lemon juice, mustard, thyme, and black pepper to make the vinaigrette.
5. Slice grilled chicken and add to the salad. Add a vinaigrette drizzle and mix to combine.

TIPS

- Chicken is a lean source of protein.
- Mixed greens and vegetables provide essential vitamins and minerals.
- Olive oil and lemon juice offer healthy fats and flavor.
- You can adjust the amount of chicken and vegetables to your liking.

NUTRITIONAL FACTS

Calories: 250

Protein: 20 grams

Carbohydrates: 5 grams

Fiber: 2 grams

Potassium: 200 milligrams

Phosphorus: 150 milligrams

Sodium: 30 milligrams

BAKED TILAPIA WITH LEMON AND HERBS

Yields: 4 servings | **Prep Time:** 5 minutes | **Cooking Time:** 15 minutes | **Serving Size:** 1 fillet

INGREDIENTS

- 4 (4-ounce) tilapia fillets
- 1 tablespoon olive oil
- 1/2 lemon, thinly sliced
- 1/4 cup chopped fresh parsley
- 1/4 teaspoon dried thyme
- Black pepper to taste

INSTRUCTIONS

1. Preheat oven to 400°F (200°C).
2. Place tilapia fillets on a baking sheet lined with parchment paper.
3. Add a little olive oil and black pepper for seasoning.
4. Top each fillet with lemon slices and sprinkle with parsley and thyme.
5. Fish should flake easily with a fork and be cooked through after Twelve to fifteen minutes of baking in the oven.

TIPS

- Fish with a mild flavour and low mercury content is tilapia, which is also an excellent source of protein.
- Lemon and herbs add flavor without the need for salt.
- Baking is a healthy cooking method that does not require added fat.

NUTRITIONAL FACTS

Calories: 150

Protein: 20 grams

Carbohydrates: 2 grams

Fiber: 0 grams

Potassium: 200 milligrams

Phosphorus: 200 milligrams

Sodium: 50 milligrams

CHICKEN MEATBALLS WITH ZUCCHINI NOODLES AND TOMATO SAUCE

Yields: 4 servings | **Prep Time:** 15 minutes | **Cooking Time:** 25 minutes | **Serving Size:** 1 cup

INGREDIENTS

- 1 pound ground chicken
- 1/4 cup chopped onion
- 1/4 cup chopped green bell pepper
- 1/4 teaspoon garlic powder
- 1/4 teaspoon onion powder
- 1/4 teaspoon black pepper
- 2 medium zucchini, spiralized into noodles
- 1 cup low-sodium tomato sauce

INSTRUCTIONS

1. Preheat oven to 375°F (190°C).
2. In a large bowl, combine ground chicken, onion, bell pepper, garlic powder, onion powder, and black pepper.
3. Form mixture into small meatballs.
4. Put the meatballs on a parchment paper-lined baking sheet.
5. Bake for between fifteen and twenty minutes, or until well done. While meatballs are baking, heat a skillet over medium heat and add zucchini noodles. Cook for 2-3 minutes, or until tender-crisp.
6. Warm tomato sauce in a separate saucepan.
7. Serve meatballs over zucchini noodles with tomato sauce.

TIPS

- Ground chicken is a lean source of protein.

- Zucchini noodles are a low-carb and low-potassium alternative to pasta.

- Use low-sodium tomato sauce to reduce sodium intake.

- You can add other vegetables to the meatballs, such as grated carrots or chopped mushrooms.

NUTRITIONAL FACTS

Calories: 300

Protein: 25 grams

Carbohydrates: 15 grams

Fiber: 4 grams

Potassium: 300 milligrams

Phosphorus: 200 milligrams

Sodium: 100 milligrams

CHICKEN FAJITAS WITH BELL PEPPERS AND ONIONS

Yields: 4 servings | **Prep time:** 15 minutes (plus marinating time) | **Cooking Time:** 15 minutes | **Serving Size:** 2 lettuce wraps

INGREDIENTS

- 1 pound boneless, skinless chicken breast, thinly sliced
- 1 tablespoon olive oil
- 1/2 teaspoon chili powder
- 1/4 teaspoon garlic powder
- 1/4 teaspoon onion powder
- 1/4 teaspoon cumin
- 1/4 teaspoon smoked paprika
- 1 green bell pepper, thinly sliced
- 1 red bell pepper, thinly sliced
- 1/2 onion, thinly sliced
- Four big leaves of lettuce (romaine or butter lettuce)

INSTRUCTIONS

1. In a bowl, combine chicken with olive oil, chili powder, garlic powder, onion powder, cumin, and smoked paprika.
2. Marinate for at least 15 minutes.
3. Heat a large skillet over medium-high heat.
4. Cook the chicken until it is thoroughly done and browned.
5. Remove chicken from skillet and set aside.

6. Add bell peppers and onions to the skillet and cook until softened, about 5-7 minutes.

7. Put the chicken back in the skillet and give it a good mix.

8. Serve chicken and vegetable mixture in lettuce leaves.

TIPS

- This recipe is a good source of lean protein and vegetables.

- For a low-carb alternative,we use lettuce leaves rather than tortillas.

- Choose low-sodium spices to keep sodium levels in check.

NUTRITIONAL FACTS

Calories: 200

Protein: 25 grams

Carbohydrates: 8 grams

Fiber: 2 grams

Potassium: 250 milligrams

Phosphorus: 150 milligrams

Sodium: 35 milligrams

SALMON WITH ROASTED BROCCOLI AND CAULIFLOWER

Yields: 4 servings | **Prep Time:** 10 minutes | **Cooking Time:** 30 minutes | **Serving Size:** 1 salmon fillet + 1 cup vegetables

INGREDIENTS

- 4 (4-ounce) salmon fillets
- 1 head broccoli, cut into florets
- 1 head cauliflower, cut into florets
- 1 tablespoon olive oil
- 1/2 teaspoon dried thyme
- 1/4 teaspoon black pepper
- Lemon wedges for serving

INSTRUCTIONS

1. Preheat oven to 400°F (200°C).
2. Toss broccoli and cauliflower florets with olive oil, thyme, and black pepper.
3. Arrange on the baking sheet in a single layer.
4. Roast for between twenty and twenty-five minutes, or until soft and beginning to turn golden.
5. Place salmon fillets on a separate baking sheet lined with parchment paper.
6. Bake for 12-15 minutes, or until cooked through.
7. Serve salmon with roasted vegetables and lemon wedges.

TIPS

- Omega-3 fatty acids, which are good for the heart, are abundant in salmon.
- Roasting brings out the natural sweetness of broccoli and cauliflower.
- Serve with lemon wedges for a refreshing flavor boost.

NUTRITIONAL FACTS

Calories: 300

Protein: 30 grams

Carbohydrates: 10 grams

Fiber: 4 grams

Potassium: 400 milligrams

Phosphorus: 300 milligrams

Sodium: 50 milligrams

LEMONY SHRIMP AND ASPARAGUS SKILLET

Yields: 4 servings | **Prep Time:** 10 minutes | **Cooking Time:** 10 minutes | **Serving Size:** 1 cup

INGREDIENTS

- 1 pound large shrimp, peeled and deveined
- One bunch of asparagus, thinly sliced into 1-inch segments
- 1 tablespoon olive oil
- 2 cloves garlic, minced
- 1/4 cup low-sodium chicken broth
- 2 tablespoons lemon juice
- 1/4 teaspoon black pepper
- 1/4 cup chopped fresh parsley

INSTRUCTIONS

1. Heat olive oil in a large skillet over medium heat.
2. Add shrimp and cook for 2-3 minutes per side, or until pink and cooked through.
3. Remove shrimp from skillet and set aside.
4. Add asparagus to the skillet and cook for 3-4 minutes, or until tender-crisp.
5. Sauté the garlic for 30 seconds, or until it becomes aromatic.
6. Stir in chicken broth, lemon juice, and black pepper.
7. Return shrimp to the skillet and cook for 1 minute more, or until heated through.
8. Stir in parsley and serve immediately.

TIPS

- Shrimp is a good source of lean protein and omega-3 fatty acids.
- Asparagus is a low-calorie and low-carb vegetable that is high in fiber and vitamins.
- Lemon juice and herbs add flavor without adding sodium.

NUTRITIONAL FACTS

Calories: 200

Protein: 25 grams

Carbohydrates: 5 grams

Fiber: 2 grams

Potassium: 250 milligrams

Phosphorus: 200 milligrams

Sodium: 100 milligrams

CHAPTER 6

SNACKS

APPLE SLICES WITH CINNAMON

Yields: 1 serving | **Prep Time:** 5 minutes | **Serving Size:** 1 medium apple

INGREDIENTS

- 1 medium apple (Granny Smith or Honeycrisp), sliced
- 1/4 teaspoon ground cinnamon

INSTRUCTIONS

1. Wash and core the apple.
2. Slice the apple into thin rounds.
3. Sprinkle cinnamon over the apple slices.
4. Enjoy it right now or save it for later in the fridge in an airtight container.

TIPS

- Apples are a good source of fiber and vitamins, and low in potassium.
- Cinnamon adds flavor without adding sodium or potassium.

NUTRITIONAL FACTS

Calories: 60

Protein: <1 gram

Carbohydrates: 15 grams

Fiber: 3 grams

Potassium: 115 milligrams

Phosphorus: 10 milligrams

Sodium: 1 milligram

CELERY STICKS WITH TUNA SALAD

Yields: 2 servings | **Prep Time:** 10 minutes | **Serving Size:** 2 celery sticks

INGREDIENTS

- 2 stalks celery, cut into 4-inch sticks
- One five-ounce can of drained tuna in water
- 1 tablespoon plain, non-fat Greek yogurt
- 1 teaspoon Dijon mustard
- 1/4 teaspoon dried dill
- Black pepper to taste

INSTRUCTIONS

1. In a small bowl, combine tuna, yogurt, mustard, dill, and black pepper.
2. Fill celery sticks with the tuna salad mixture.

TIPS

- This snack is a good source of lean protein and low in carbohydrates.
- Celery is a low-calorie and hydrating vegetable.
- Plain, non-fat Greek yogurt is a healthier alternative to mayonnaise.
- Use tuna packed in water to avoid added sodium.

NUTRITIONAL FACTS

Calories: 100

Protein: 15 grams

Carbohydrates: 2 grams

Fiber: 1 gram

Potassium: 150 milligrams

Phosphorus: 100 milligrams

Sodium: 50 milligrams

MIXED BERRY BOWL

Yields: 1 serving | **Prep Time:** 5 minutes | **Serving Size:** 1 cup

INGREDIENTS

- 1/2 cup blueberries
- 1/2 cup raspberries
- 1/2 cup sliced strawberries

INSTRUCTIONS

1. Wash and dry all berries.
2. Combine berries in a bowl.

TIPS

- This snack is packed with antioxidants, vitamins, and fiber.
- It is naturally low in potassium, phosphorus, and sodium.
- If desired, you can add a small dollop of plain, non-fat Greek yogurt for extra protein.

NUTRITIONAL FACTS

Calories: 50

Protein: 1 gram

Carbohydrates: 12 grams

Fiber: 4 grams

Potassium: 140 milligrams

Phosphorus: 20 milligrams

Sodium: 1 milligram

HARD-BOILED EGG WHITES WITH HERBS AND SPICES

Yields: 1 serving | **Prep Time:** 5 minutes | **Cooking Time:** 11 minutes | **Serving Size:** 2 egg whites

INGREDIENTS

- 2 large egg whites
- 1/4 teaspoon dried dill
- 1/4 teaspoon onion powder
- Pinch of black pepper

INSTRUCTIONS

1. Place egg whites in a saucepan and cover with cold water.
2. Bring water to a boil, then reduce heat to low and simmer for 1 minute.
3. Take off the heat, put a lid on it, and wait ten minutes.
4. Drain and peel eggs.
5. Chop egg whites and place in a bowl.
6. Sprinkle it with dill, onion powder, and black pepper.
7. Toss gently to combine.

TIPS

- Egg whites are a good source of low-phosphorus protein.
- To enhance flavour without adding salt, we use herbs and spices.
- Avoid using the yolk, as it is high in phosphorus.

NUTRITIONAL FACTS

Calories: 35

Protein: 7 grams

Carbohydrates: 0 grams

Fiber: 0 grams

Potassium: 55 milligrams

Phosphorus: 25 milligrams

Sodium: 15 milligrams

CUCUMBER SLICES WITH LEMON-DILL DIP

Yields: 1 serving | **Prep Time:** 5 minutes | **Serving Size:** 1 cucumber and 1/4 cup dip

INGREDIENTS

- 1 cucumber, thinly sliced
- 1/4 cup plain, non-fat Greek yogurt
- 1 tablespoon chopped fresh dill (or 1 teaspoon dried dill)
- 1 tablespoon lemon juice
- Black pepper to taste

INSTRUCTIONS

1. In a small bowl, combine Greek yogurt, dill, lemon juice, and black pepper.
2. Serve with cucumber slices for dipping.

TIPS

- Cucumbers are a hydrating and low-calorie vegetable.
- Plain, non-fat Greek yogurt is a good source of protein and probiotics.
- Fresh dill adds flavor without adding sodium.

NUTRITIONAL FACTS

Calories: 50

Protein: 5 grams

Carbohydrates: 5 grams

Fiber: 1 gram

Potassium: 150 milligrams

Phosphorus: 50 milligrams

Sodium: 15 milligrams

ROASTED EDAMAME WITH SPICES

Yields: 2 servings | **Prep Time:** 5 minutes | **Cooking Time:** 10-12 minutes | **Serving Size:** 1/2 cup

INGREDIENTS

- 1 cup frozen shelled edamame, thawed
- 1/2 teaspoon olive oil
- 1/4 teaspoon garlic powder
- 1/4 teaspoon onion powder
- 1/4 teaspoon smoked paprika

INSTRUCTIONS

1. Preheat the oven to 400°F (200°C).
2. In a bowl, toss edamame with olive oil, garlic powder, onion powder, and smoked paprika.
3. Arrange the edamame on a baking sheet in one layer.
4. Roast for 10-12 minutes, or until lightly browned and crispy.

TIPS

- Edamame is a good source of plant-based protein and fiber.
- Roasting enhances the flavor and texture of the edamame.
- Choose unsalted edamame to avoid excess sodium.
- This recipe is naturally low in potassium and phosphorus.

NUTRITIONAL FACTS

Calories: 120

Protein: 12 grams

Carbohydrates: 8 grams

Fiber: 4 grams

Potassium: 160 milligrams

Phosphorus: 100 milligrams

Sodium: 5 milligrams

CHIA SEED PUDDING WITH BERRIES

Yields: 1 serving | **Prep Time:** 5 minutes | **Refrigeration Time:** 4 hours minimum | **Serving Size:** 1 cup

INGREDIENTS

- ¼ cup chia seeds
- 1 cup unsweetened rice milk
- ½ teaspoon vanilla extract
- ¼ teaspoon ground cinnamon (optional)
- ½ cup mixed berries (blueberries, raspberries, sliced strawberries)

INSTRUCTIONS

1. In a jar or container, whisk together chia seeds, rice milk, vanilla extract, and cinnamon (if using).
2. Refrigerate for at least 4 hours or overnight, until the pudding thickens.
3. Top with mixed berries before serving

TIPS

- Chia seeds are an excellent source of fiber and omega-3 fatty acids, both beneficial for heart health.
- Rice milk is a low-potassium and low-phosphorus alternative to dairy milk.
- Berries add natural sweetness, antioxidants, and vitamins.
- This pudding is a great source of fiber, helping to regulate blood sugar and promote satiety.

NUTRITIONAL FACTS

Calories: 150

Protein: 5 grams

Carbohydrates: 18 grams

Fiber: 11 grams

Potassium: 120 milligrams

Phosphorus: 50 milligrams

Sodium: 10 milligrams

EGG SALAD WITH WHOLE WHEAT CRACKERS

Yields: 1 serving | **Prep Time:** 5 minutes | **Serving Size:** 1/2 cup egg salad and 4 crackers

INGREDIENTS

- 2 hard-boiled egg whites, chopped
- 1 tablespoon plain, non-fat Greek yogurt
- 1 teaspoon Dijon mustard
- 1/4 teaspoon dried dill
- Black pepper to taste
- 4 whole wheat crackers

INSTRUCTIONS

1. In a small bowl, combine chopped egg whites, yogurt, mustard, dill, and black pepper.
2. Mash with a fork until combined.
3. Serve with whole wheat crackers.

TIPS

- Using only egg whites reduces phosphorus content.
- Plain, non-fat Greek yogurt replaces mayonnaise, lowering fat and calories while adding protein.
- Limit whole wheat crackers to a few to manage carbohydrate intake.

NUTRITIONAL FACTS

Calories: 100

Protein: 10 grams

Carbohydrates: 8 grams

Fiber: 2 grams

Potassium: 70 milligrams

Phosphorus: 80 milligrams

Sodium: 100 milligrams

COTTAGE CHEESE WITH CINNAMON AND BERRIES

Yields: 1 serving | **Prep Time:** 5 minutes | **Serving Size:** 1 cup

INGREDIENTS

- 1/2 cup low-sodium cottage cheese
- 1/4 teaspoon ground cinnamon
- 1/2 cup mixed berries (blueberries, raspberries, sliced strawberries)

INSTRUCTIONS

1. In a small bowl, combine cottage cheese and cinnamon.
2. Top with mixed berries.

TIPS

- Choose low-sodium cottage cheese to manage sodium intake.
- This snack is a good source of protein and calcium.
- Berries add natural sweetness and antioxidants.
- If you prefer, you can substitute the berries with a small diced pear for a different flavor profile.

NUTRITIONAL FACTS

Calories: 100

Protein: 14 grams

Carbohydrates: 8 grams

Fiber: 2 grams

Potassium: 120 milligrams

Phosphorus: 150 milligrams

Sodium: 120 milligrams

SPICED ROASTED CAULIFLOWER

Yields: 4 servings | **Prep Time:** 10 minutes | **Cooking Time:** 20-25 minutes | **Serving Size:** 1 cup

INGREDIENTS

- 1 head cauliflower, cut into florets
- 1 tablespoon olive oil
- 1/2 teaspoon paprika
- 1/4 teaspoon garlic powder
- 1/4 teaspoon onion powder
- 1/4 teaspoon cumin
- Black pepper to taste

INSTRUCTIONS

1. Preheat oven to 400°F (200°C).
2. In a large bowl, toss cauliflower florets with olive oil, paprika, garlic powder, onion powder, cumin, and black pepper.
3. Arrange the cauliflower on a baking pan in one layer.
4. Roast for 20-25 minutes, or until tender and lightly browned, flipping halfway through.

TIPS

- Cauliflower is a low-calorie, low-carbohydrate vegetable that is high in fiber and vitamin C.
- Roasting cauliflower caramelizes the edges and brings out its inherent sweetness.
- Spices add flavor without adding sodium.

NUTRITIONAL FACTS

Calories: 70

Protein: 2 grams

Carbohydrates: 6 grams

Fiber: 3 grams

Potassium: 160 milligrams

Phosphorus: 50 milligrams

Sodium: 10 milligrams

CUCUMBER SALAD WITH LEMON AND HERBS

Yields: 2 servings | **Prep Time:** 5 minutes | **Serving Size:** 1/2 cup

INGREDIENTS

- 1 cucumber, thinly sliced
- 1/4 cup chopped fresh herbs (such as dill, parsley, or mint)
- 1 tablespoon lemon juice
- 1/4 teaspoon black pepper

INSTRUCTIONS

1. In a bowl, combine cucumber slices, herbs, lemon juice, and black pepper.
2. Toss gently to coat.

TIPS

- This salad is refreshing, hydrating, and very low in calories and carbohydrates.
- Vitamins and minerals can be found in abundance in cucumbers.
- Fresh herbs add flavor and nutrients.
- Lemon juice adds a bright and tangy flavor without adding sodium.

NUTRITIONAL FACTS

Calories: 20

Protein: 1 gram

Carbohydrates: 3 grams

Fiber: 1 gram

Potassium: 100 milligrams

Phosphorus: 15 milligrams

Sodium: 5 milligrams

BELL PEPPER SLICES WITH LOW-SODIUM HUMMUS

Yields: 2 servings | **Prep Time:** 5 minutes | **Serving Size:** 1/2 bell pepper and 1/4 cup hummus

INGREDIENTS

- 1 red bell pepper, seeded and cut into strips
- One green bell pepper, peeled and sliced into thin pieces
- 1/2 cup low-sodium hummus

INSTRUCTIONS

1. Arrange bell pepper slices on a plate.
2. Serve with hummus for dipping.

TIPS

- Vitamins A and C are found in bell peppers in considerable amounts.
- Hummus is a good source of plant-based protein and fiber.
- Choose a low-sodium hummus to limit sodium intake.
- This is a healthy and satisfying snack or appetizer.

NUTRITIONAL FACTS

Calories: 150

Protein: 5 grams

Carbohydrates: 15 grams

Fiber: 5 grams

Potassium: 200 milligrams

Phosphorus: 50 milligrams

Sodium: 100 milligrams (depending on the hummus brand)

TUNA SALAD LETTUCE CUPS

Yields: 4 servings | **Prep Time:** 10 minutes | **Serving Size:** 1 lettuce cup

INGREDIENTS

- 5 ounces can tuna in water, drained
- 1/4 cup finely chopped celery
- 1 tablespoon plain, non-fat Greek yogurt
- 1 teaspoon Dijon mustard
- 1/4 teaspoon dried dill
- Black pepper to taste
- Four huge leaves of lettuce (romaine or butter lettuce)

INSTRUCTIONS

1. In a medium bowl, combine tuna, celery, yogurt, mustard, dill, and black pepper.
2. Gently toss to combine.
3. Spoon tuna salad into the centre of each lettuce leaf, dividing it equally.
4. Fold or roll up the lettuce leaves to enclose the tuna salad.

TIPS

- This recipe is a good source of lean protein and omega-3 fatty acids.
- Plain, non-fat Greek yogurt is a healthier alternative to mayonnaise, providing protein and probiotics.
- Use fresh dill for optimal flavor.
- The quantity of ingredients can be changed to suit your tastes.
- For added taste, pour in some lemon juice.

Calories: 100

Protein: 15 grams

Carbohydrates: 2 grams

Fiber: 1 gram

Potassium: 150 milligrams

Phosphorus: 100 milligrams

Sodium: 45 milligrams

APPLE AND CELERY SALAD WITH LEMON DRESSING

Yields: 2 servings | **Prep Time:** 10 minutes | **Serving Size**: 1 cup

INGREDIENTS

- 2 apples (e.g., Granny Smith or Honeycrisp), diced
- 2 stalks celery, thinly sliced
- 1 tablespoon olive oil
- 2 tablespoons lemon juice
- 1/4 teaspoon dried thyme
- Black pepper to taste

INSTRUCTIONS

1. In a medium bowl, combine diced apples, celery, and chopped herbs (if using).
2. In a separate small bowl, whisk together olive oil, lemon juice, thyme, and black pepper to make the dressing.
3. Drizzle the salad with the dressing and mix to combine.

TIPS

- Apples and celery are low in potassium and high in fiber.
- The lemon dressing adds brightness and flavor without added sodium.
- If desired, you can add a small amount of chopped walnuts for extra protein and healthy fats.

NUTRITIONAL FACTS

Calories: 100

Protein: 1 gram

Carbohydrates: 12 grams

Fiber: 4 grams

Potassium: 200 milligrams

Phosphorus: 20 milligrams

Sodium: 5 milligrams

ROASTED CAULIFLOWER HUMMUS

Yields: 4 servings | **Prep Time:** 10 minutes | **Cooking Time:** 20-25 minutes | **Serving Size:** 1/4 cup

INGREDIENTS

- 1 head cauliflower, cut into florets
- 1 tablespoon olive oil
- 1/2 teaspoon cumin
- 1/4 teaspoon paprika
- 1/4 cup tahini (sesame seed paste)
- 2 tablespoons lemon juice
- 1/4 cup water
- Black pepper to taste

INSTRUCTIONS

1. Preheat the oven to 400°F (200°C).
2. Combine paprika, cumin, and olive oil with the cauliflower florets.
3. Spread cauliflower on a baking sheet and roast for 20-25 minutes, or until tender and lightly browned.
4. In a food processor, combine roasted cauliflower, tahini, lemon juice, and water.
5. Blend until smooth, adding additional water as necessary.
6. Season with black pepper to taste.

- This hummus is a healthier and lower-potassium alternative to traditional hummus made with chickpeas.

- Vitamin C and fiber can be found in abundance in cauliflower.

- Tahini adds protein and healthy fats.

- Lemon juice adds flavor without adding sodium.

- Serve with celery sticks, carrot sticks, or bell pepper slices for a healthy snack or appetizer.

NUTRITIONAL FACTS

Calories: 120

Protein: 5 grams

Carbohydrates: 10 grams

Fiber: 4 grams

Potassium: 200 milligrams

Phosphorus: 100 milligrams

Sodium: 50 milligrams (depending on the tahini brand)

CHAPTER 7

14 DAYS MEAL PLANS

Week	Day	Breakfast	Lunch	Dinner	Snacks
1	1	Berry Chia Seed Pudding with Rice Milk	Tuna Salad with Celery and Grapes on Lettuce	Baked Chicken with Rosemary and Roasted Vegetables	Apple Slices with Cinnamon
	2	Scrambled Egg Whites with Spinach and Herbs	Salmon with Roasted Cauliflower and Lemon-Dill Sauce	Baked Cod with Lemon and Herbs	Celery Sticks with Tuna Salad
	3	Raspberry and Rice Milk Smoothie	Lemony Chicken Soup with Herbs	Chicken and Vegetable Curry with Cauliflower Rice	Mixed Berry Bowl
	4	Tofu Scramble with Turmeric and Vegetables	Tuna Salad Lettuce Cups	Shrimp Scampi with Zucchini Noodles	Hard-Boiled Eggs with Herbs and Spices
	5	Pear and Ginger Oatmeal	Chicken and Vegetable Stir-Fry with Cauliflower Rice	Lemon Herb Roasted Chicken with Roasted Vegetables	Cucumber Slices with Lemon-Dill Dip
	6	Egg White Salad with Mixed	Cucumber and Bell Pepper Salad with	One-Pan Baked Salmon with	Roasted Edamame with Spices

		Greens and Herbs	Lemon-Herb Vinaigrette	Asparagus and Zucchini	
	7	Berry Parfait with Coconut Yogurt	Quinoa Salad with Black Beans and Lemon Vinaigrette	Tofu Stir-Fry with Vegetables and Cauliflower Rice	Chia Seed Pudding with Berries
2	8	Spinach and Mushroom Omelet	Turkey Lettuce Wraps with Spicy Yogurt Sauce	Grilled Chicken Salad with Lemon-Herb Vinaigrette	Apple Slices with Cinnamon
	9	Cauliflower "Oatmeal" with Berries and Cinnamon	Zucchini Noodles with Pesto and Grilled Chicken	Baked Tilapia with Lemon and Herbs	Cottage Cheese with Cinnamon and Berries
	10	Salmon Cakes with Dill Yogurt Sauce	Cauliflower Rice Bowl with Shrimp and Vegetables	Chicken Meatballs with Zucchini Noodles and Tomato Sauce	Egg Salad with Whole Wheat Crackers
	11	Lemony Asparagus and Tofu Scramble	Spinach Salad with Grilled Chicken and Balsamic Vinaigrette	Chicken Fajitas with Bell Peppers and Onions	Spiced Roasted Cauliflower
	12	Broccoli and Egg White Muffins	Lemony Chickpea Salad with Fresh Herbs	Salmon with Roasted Broccoli and Cauliflower	Cucumber Salad with Lemon and Herbs
	13	Oatmeal with Pear and Spices	Baked Fish Tacos with Cabbage Slaw	Lemony Shrimp and Asparagus Skillet	Bell Pepper Slices with Hummus (low sodium)

	14	Tuna Salad with Whole Wheat Crackers	Broccoli and Chicken Soup	Veggie Burger on a Lettuce Bun with Mustard	Apple and Celery Salad with Lemon Dressing

FREQUENTLY ASKED QUESTIONS FAQs

1. What is a diabetic renal diet?

- A diabetic renal diet is a meal plan designed for people with both diabetes and chronic kidney disease (CKD). It focuses on limiting sodium, potassium, phosphorus, and protein, while also managing carbohydrate intake to control blood sugar levels.

2. Why is a diabetic renal diet important?

- This diet helps to slow down the progression of kidney disease, manage diabetes complications, and prevent fluid buildup in the body. It also aims to provide adequate nutrition for overall health.

3. What foods should I limit or avoid on a diabetic renal diet?

- High-sodium foods: Processed foods, canned soups, cured meats, salted snacks, soy sauce.
- High-potassium foods: Bananas, oranges, potatoes, tomatoes, dairy products.
- High-phosphorus foods: Nuts, seeds, whole grains, dairy products.
- High-protein foods (in later stages of CKD): Red meat, poultry, fish, eggs.

4. What foods can I eat on a diabetic renal diet?

- Low-sodium fruits and vegetables: Apples, berries, cauliflower, cucumber, bell peppers.
- Low-potassium fruits and vegetables: Grapes, blueberries, cabbage, green beans, onions.
- Lean protein: Fish, skinless poultry, egg whites, beans (in moderation).
- Healthy fats: Olive oil, avocado, unsalted nuts (in moderation).
- Limited carbohydrates: Whole grains (in moderation), berries, non-starchy vegetables.

5. How much sodium, potassium, and phosphorus can I have per day?

- This will depend on your individual needs and the stage of your kidney disease. Consult your doctor or a registered dietitian for specific recommendations.

6. Can I still enjoy desserts on a diabetic renal diet?

- Yes, but in moderation. Look for desserts made with sugar substitutes and limit high-potassium fruits like bananas and oranges.

7. Can I eat out while on a diabetic renal diet?

- Yes, but it requires careful planning. Choose restaurants that offer healthier options and ask about ingredients and preparation methods to ensure your meal is low in sodium, potassium, and phosphorus.

8. Do I need to take any supplements on this diet?

- Your doctor may recommend vitamin and mineral supplements, as some nutrients may be restricted on this diet.

9. What are some tips for following a diabetic renal diet?

- Read food labels carefully.
- Plan your meals in advance.
- Cook at home more often.
- Choose fresh or frozen produce over canned.
- Use herbs and spices for flavor instead of salt.

10. Can I drink alcohol on a diabetic renal diet?

- Alcohol should be limited or avoided, as it can affect blood sugar levels and may worsen kidney function.

11. Is a diabetic renal diet complicated?

- It may seem overwhelming at first, but with planning and support, it can become a healthy lifestyle choice.

12. Can a diabetic renal diet help me lose weight?

- It's not a weight loss diet, but following it can lead to weight loss if you're overweight or obese.

13. Can I still be physically active on a diabetic renal diet?

- Yes, regular exercise is important for managing both diabetes and CKD.

- Before beginning any new fitness plan, speak with your physician.

14. How often should I see my doctor or dietitian?

- Regular checkups are essential to monitor your kidney function, blood sugar levels, and overall health. Your doctor or dietitian can adjust your diet plan as needed.

15. Where can I find more information and support?

- Speak with your physician or a qualified dietitian.

- Join a support group for people with CKD and diabetes.

- Search online for reliable resources and recipes.

CONCLUSION

As we close the pages of this culinary journey, I want to express my heartfelt gratitude for joining me on this exploration of flavor, health, and well-being. It's been a pleasure to share these recipes and tips, designed to make your life with CKD stage 4 and type 2 diabetes a little bit easier, and a whole lot more delicious.

Remember, food is not just sustenance; it's a source of joy, connection, and nourishment for both body and soul. Embracing a diabetic renal diet doesn't mean sacrificing taste or enjoyment. It simply means discovering new ways to savor the incredible flavors that nature has to offer while prioritizing your health.

As you continue on your culinary adventure, remember that small changes can make a big difference. Experiment with new ingredients, try out different flavor combinations, and most importantly, listen to your body. Your journey with food is uniquely yours, and I encourage you to personalize these recipes and make them your own.

If you have any questions or would like to share your experiences with these recipes, please don't hesitate to reach out. Your feedback is invaluable to me.

I hope this cookbook has empowered you to take charge of your health and rediscover the joy of cooking. Here's to your continued well-being, and may your kitchen always be filled with delicious aromas and the warmth of good food shared with loved ones.

Thank you for reading, and bon appétit!

Made in the USA
Monee, IL
27 October 2024

68755820R00085